THE ReSET

An Elevated Discipline

Pausing, Pivoting, and Forward Stance

TRACEY GREENE-WASHINGTON

THE RESET
An Elevated Discipline: Pausing, Pivoting, and Forward Stance

GREENE-WASHINGTON, TRACEY, Author
THE RESET
TRACEY GREENE-WASHINGTON

Published by:
ELITE ONLINE PUBLISHING
63 East 11400 South
Suite #230
Sandy, UT 84070
EliteOnlinePublishing.com

ISBN: 978-1-971310-03-9 (ePub)
ISBN: 978-1-971310-04-6 (Paperback)

LCCN: 2025928092

SEL031000
PHI015000

All rights reserved by TRACEY GREENE-WASHINGTON
This book is printed in the United States of America.

Editing and publishing support provided by The Write Image Consulting, LLC and Write Your Life.

PRAISES FOR
TRACEY GREENE-WASHINGTON

After pursuing purposeful alignment, the journey doesn't necessarily get easier; it often becomes harder. It requires a deeper level of patience, grace, and intentionality to navigate the whirlwind of emotions, shifting priorities, and external pressures that come with real change. This vital next step is the bridge between awareness and sustainability, the space where you learn to protect what you've discovered and nurture it into something lasting. *The ReSET* invites you to pause long enough to truly see, to pivot with courage when the path shifts, and to take a forward stance grounded in clarity and conviction. This isn't about perfection; it's about presence. It's about building the capacity to stay rooted in purpose while adapting to the ever-changing realities of life and leadership. Because after pursuing alignment comes the real work: learning how to live it, maintain it, and keep evolving through it.

~ Ryan Francis
Lawyer and Entrepreneur, LuvSeas Tours

In this book, Tracey intertwines powerful lessons in her stories, takes us through a tough journey, and offers permission to fail and adapt at every step. The best part: She holds your hand through it all!

~ Garima Grupta
Managing Director, Corus International

This book offers a rare combination of vulnerability and presence that invites the reader into a deep pause, one that asks you to be more vulnerable and present with yourself. It calls you into truths that you might have shielded yourself from, yet you need to face. From the messy middle to the forward stance, this journey offers more than a set of curious exercises; it offers embodied transformation and a clear understanding of purpose. You can be a leader or a follower. This book is for leaders.

~ Jazmin Francesca
CEO, Jazmin Rogers, LLC

The ReSET is a compelling call to adopt transformational leadership through deliberate pauses and intentional realignment. Once again, Tracey skillfully guides readers through a reset journey that offers both philosophical insights and practical tools to manage the complexities of personal and professional growth. This book is crucial for leaders and changemakers eager to examine their habits, elevate their methods, and fully embrace their roles as agents of meaningful change.

~ Kristy Teskey
Innovation Catalyst, Faster Glass

In my forty years serving as a C-Suite Executive, woman business owner, and now as a consultant, my passion and purpose have always centered on elevating women and working closely with visionary men who understand that true progress evokes mutual energy and alignment of purpose. Through this journey, I have learned that success without alignment is fleeting, and that we must live in purposeful alignment.

A woman business colleague recently introduced me to the Japanese concept of ikigai, the intersection of passion, mission, vocation, and profession. It is a powerful compass. Yet, as Tracey Greene-Washington so eloquently reveals in *The ReSET*, knowing your purpose isn't enough. Choosing alignment is not enough; you must embody it.

Tracey invites us to ReSET, to pause, pivot, and propel ourselves into a new narrative that reflects who we are becoming, not who we have been. Her wisdom challenges us to shed outdated stories, embrace intentional transformation, and lead with clarity, courage, and conviction. Thank you, Tracey, for guiding us to the next level and for showing that alignment is not a destination, but a disciplined, evolving practice of becoming our highest self.

~ Betty Hines
CEO & Founder, Women Elevating Women (W.E.W.)

This book holds the power to shape a new mindset in readers, one that guides you into a new embodied forward stance. Tracey's insights have enlightened me and helped move me to prioritize self-care and self-focus. With a new perspective on my challenges (redefining what's hard for me) and my opportunities (strategies that keep me consistent), I know I can create my own unapologetic stance that the world will see.

~ Julia Darity
Youth Leader and Advocate

As a nonprofit leader and friend for more than fifteen years, I have witnessed Tracey's evolution through a variety of complex personal and professional challenges. She has emerged as an adaptive, insightful, and powerful leader. In vivid detail on the pages of this book, Tracey provides a roadmap for the journey of transformation, reflecting a daunting landscape of twists, turns, and uncharted territories. Yet, she provides assurance from firsthand experience that there is purpose and hope in every step. For anyone undergoing your own life challenges, this is a comprehensive account of how to navigate through.

~ Marcus Walton
President & CEO, Grantmakers for Effective Organizations

Take the Purposeful Alignment Survey

Your First Yes...

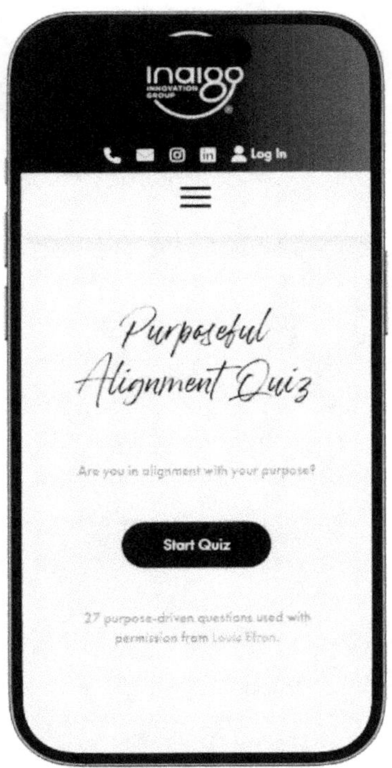

A valuable resource to discover where you are on your journey and to ReSET towards purposeful alignment.

https://indigoinnovationgroup.com/purposeful-alignment-quiz/

Tracey Greene-Washington

SPARK INNOVATION. CULTIVATE CHANGE.

indigo
INNOVATION GROUP
®

Take this free survey to get to your first YES!

To the countless Southern leaders and women representing a range of beautiful hues, positionalities, backgrounds, and sectors, who opened doors and created intentional seats and space for me along my leadership journey.

To those who taught me how to use my voice and applied soothing balm in the form of love, tough lessons, support, elevation, and leadership.

You taught me how to get proximal to listen, learn, have bold conversations, and, most importantly, be of service toward stewarding valuable resources, holding powerful spaces, and transforming the world.

TABLE OF CONTENTS

ELEVATED DISCIPLINE 1:
The Power of the Pause

ELEVATED DISCIPLINE 3:
Embodiment: The Forward Stance

THE RESET: PROPOSITION ACCEPTED

This book is a calling forward of new, emerging, and seasoned game changers who accepted the powerful proposition to choose purposeful alignment. Purposeful alignment is unwavering clarity regarding your unique assignment or calling in spaces, relationships, initiatives, communities, and institutions. This type of clarity couples with the intentional and strategic activation and positioning of your voice, unique role, gifts, and experiences to drive momentous change, impact, and transformation.

You either began this journey with the first book, *Choosing Purposeful Alignment: The Messy Middle of Transformation*, or as an individual grappling with and interrogating what it means to live on purpose, intentionally, in every aspect of your life, every day. Now, you find yourself at a critical inflection point, asking two powerful questions: What happens after I choose purposeful alignment? and What happens after I choose to become a game changer?

These questions serve as important catalysts as you travel this journey. They reveal the moments of celebration, moments of feeling paralyzed, and moments when you question your choice to reposition yourself for embodiment of purposeful alignment as a seamless part of your walk. These powerful moments of reflection, revelation, and celebration are all important layers of the messy middle, the space between where you currently are and where you desire to be. This space and these iterative questions push you to practice and normalize a new way of being in your personal and professional life. By accepting this proposition, you are being called forward and invited to reposition yourself into an elevated journey of embodiment called The ReSET.

The ReSET is not a hard stop. Instead, it is an intentional pause, pivot, and movement into a Forward Stance designed to reset your story. At this critical moment, you are called to cultivate an elevated practice of awareness, permission, choice, and strategic action to interrupt patterns in your story that have created barriers to true embodiment of your purpose. Here, you are challenged to interrogate and understand your Now Story. Next, you're called to reposition and elevate your new story by unleashing new thinking, visioning, and a sacred space to own all your layers. You do this by digging deep into your "I" work, the very personal and internal, often unspoken, work. This work guides you toward an insatiable drive to play your unique position in ecosystems of change, organizations, companies, communities, systems, and institutions to facilitate transformational impact.

The journey to ReSET gives you permission to craft a more complete story and embrace or disrupt countless mini stories that reveal themselves along the way. While doing this work, you sharpen your ability to resist quick reactions, embrace a practice of patience that allows you to wait for things to be revealed, and discover new muscles to view each experience as information without judgment. As a result, you inform intentional and powerful choices along the way that propel you forward.

By grappling with the layers of your story, you create a more complete narrative. This requires you to embrace the disruption that will ultimately emerge and view it as good medicine. By doing so, you create the space to interrogate the five basic elements of your story: the characters, the settings, the plot, the conflict, and the resolution. The interrogation brings new questions to the surface as you make power choices from a different vantage point. Consequently, you set the stage to stand in your power, to reset your story, and to embody purposeful alignment. Now, you can assume a game-changer posture, in an unapologetic and bold way, with an elevated discipline.

Through the elevated disciplines of Pausing, Pivoting, and Embodying a Forward Stance, you intentionally ReSET each component of your story. As you ReSET, you invariably elevate your posture and shift from *choosing* to *embodying* purposeful alignment. This new stance explicitly sets the stage for new choice points that will be necessary as you notice, name, persist through, and embrace the disequilibrium that can come with this new movement.

You begin to activate your agency and power, while owning, and amplifying your unique story. This is where purpose and alignment are anchored. The calling forward process moves you to a new level of leadership. Here, you shift your mindset, accountability, discomfort, disorientation, emotional stamina, and clarity, further positioning you and driving you to choose significance and transformational impact over mere success.

As you read this book, I invite you to give yourself the gift of revealing all your layers to the world, normalizing your new and evolved story. Land in a place where you trust yourself, where you are clear, bold, and prepared to take strategic action. Be grounded in a sacred place of knowing your story and standing in it, unapologetically. Understand that you must constantly work to evolve, and be committed to activating every resource at your disposal to drive innovation and transformational change. There are reminders along the way to assist you.

The intentional principles outlined in *Choosing Purposeful Alignment* are the very reminders needed: The Power of Permission, Leaning Into Transformation, and Become a Game Changer. The ReSET Journey builds upon the principles from *Choosing Purposeful Alignment* and serves as a catalyst for you to embody and reposition your posture throughout the journey. It's important to orient yourself or review the key points, concepts, and tools from *Choosing Purposeful Alignment*. Use the At-A-Glance guide on page xx, or find the book at https://www.indigoinnovationgroup.com/choosing-purposeful-alignment.

Use that book as a critical resource to acknowledge the messy middle as a transformational and cyclical process. Be grounded in the truth that you're continuously moving toward purposeful alignment. Lean into new, noticing opportunities, embrace new tools and muscles, and explore new moments that uniquely position you as a game changer to drive greater impact, strategic action, and leaderful movements.

These foundational concepts, along with the new embodiment mindset, The ReSET tools, and the stories, are meant to evoke new questions that enable you to make intentional choices as you move forward. Your journey will reveal necessary questions designed to gauge your readiness to lean into the work required to embody your evolved stance and boldly assume the posture of a game changer. As such, it is imperative that as you accept this proposition, you fully commit to this journey. First, download the accompanying digital PDF notebook using the QR code on the next page, or purchase an interactive digital version online to complete all the exercises woven throughout this book. Next, create intentional time to reflect on all the questions posed to reposition you in just the right way.

If you're ready to challenge your thinking, move through your feelings, and activate yourself to action, I'm ready to guide you.

Let the journey begin.

Scan the QR code to download the free ReSET Digital Notebook, a guided companion for your ReSET Journey.

"You are being called into something bigger than yourself."

Purposeful alignment is unwavering clarity regarding your unique assignment or calling in spaces, relationships, initiatives, communities, and institutions.

CHOICE 1: EMBRACE THE POWER OF PERMISSION

Creating space for stillness and reflection. It's an essential step that requires us to examine the concept of permission and its relationship with power-- both on an individual and collective level.

You have the power to interrupt practices, beliefs, and spaces, or relationships that no longer serve your journey by grappling with three choice points:

- Permission Principle I: Noticing the Signals and Signs
- Permission Principle II: Say "Yes"
- Permission Priinciple III: Embrace Positive Disruption and Activate Your Power

CHOICE 2: LEAN INTO TRANSFORMATION

Focus on embracing change with intention and courage. It requires us to acknowledge both the discomfort and the restorative power of transformation, understanding that growth happens in the stretch and stages-- individually, interpersonally institutionally/work, and your everyday walk.

- Transformation Principle I: Repositioning Your Stance
- Transformation Principle II: Embrace Respite and Healing
- Transformation Priinciple III: Centering Yourself
- Transformation Principle IV: Retoor and Experiment

CHOICE 3: BECOME A GAME CHANGER

You intentionally align your values with your actions. You solidly anchor yourself in your faith to reach your desired state. Your ultimate goal is to move from success to significance. Being a game changer requires a commitment to self-discovery, and by continuing to grow and deepen your relationships, you create an environment for more impactful work.

- Game Changer Principle I: Reset Your Narrative
- Game Changer Principle II: Reintroduce Yourself
- Game Changer Priinciple III: Celebrate

THE INVITATION

1. Commit to being purposefully aligned.
2. Commit to reset where neccessary.
3. Commit to your flow.

CHAPTER 1

THE BIG QUESTION: WHAT HAPPENS NEXT?

What happens after I choose to become a game changer?
What happens after I choose purposeful alignment?

You might have asked yourself these questions after walking through the three choices in Choosing Purposeful Alignment: The Messy Middle of Transformation:

Or perhaps you explored them on your individual journey of grappling with your personal purpose and your why. These are big questions that require in-depth answers, and they are the right place to start as you begin the journey of The ReSET.

I was texting with my colleague Ryan. He had been on a yearlong transformational experience that allowed him to unapologetically commit and fully lean into the journey of choosing purposeful alignment. In the text conversation, Ryan shared stories of the incremental, critical, and often hard choices he had to make as he moved through the messy middle toward purposeful alignment. His powerful words painted a vivid roadmap of his experience and explained how he had wrestled with the power of permission. He described how he made the decision to surrender to it and redefine permission for himself. He then invited me into his process to explore what leaning into transformation could look like for him.

Ryan named the discomfort and the key yeses and noes he was choosing as part of this proposition by sitting with the yes map at each of the three choices in *Choosing Purposeful Alignment*—Embrace the Power of Permission, Lean Into Transformation, and Become a Game Changer. Then, he named and moved me through an intense inflection point where he deeply considered what it meant to be a game changer in his personal and professional life. He named a new excitement he admitted was hard to put into words, calling out a profound freedom of asking, "What if?" I invited him to yield to the moment. He expressed feeling a deep and unfamiliar tingling throughout his body, possibly a long-forgotten emotion he needed to remember.

Lastly, Ryan named a profound peace and freedom that moved over him when he finally chose to lean into becoming a game changer and move toward purposeful alignment. He admitted to a heightened awareness and even a fear of naming what would be required of him as he chose purposeful alignment. As his texts came to a close, I was drawn to the last sentences: *What happens after I choose to become a game changer? What happens after I choose purposeful alignment?* These two powerful questions served as an important acknowledgement that he was at a new depth in his personal journey.

The space between the last question mark and my response was less than a second. I didn't wait to get clarity. I immediately called Ryan. Skipping any polite greetings, my response was clear and direct: "You now have to embody purposeful alignment in every moment, relationship, space, institution, and complex social issue. You must intentionally adjust your posture and stance in such a powerful way that you embody being a game changer. As a result, you'll uniquely position yourself to change, elevate, and level up the game."

That was my invitation to Ryan. And this is my invitation to you.

In *Choosing Purposeful Alignment*, I introduced the power of repositioning your posture and stance. Posture is the way you hold your body while sitting, standing, or moving. Stance is your physical orientation to the world. More specifically, it positions you to be clear about what you want to do, what is standing in your way, and prepares you to move into action.

> The game is any story, complex issue, system, lever, circumstance, relationship, or space that must be innovated, interrupted, evolved, dismantled, or configured in service to deep impact and transformational change.

In the process of embodying purposeful alignment, you not only move from repositioning your posture, but you also begin to adjust your stance and eventually embody it.

Embodiment. the explicit process of giving concrete form to an abstract concept, is the personification of an idea. Embodiment moves you—mentally, emotionally, and physically—from the proposition of what could be possible into the actualization, normalization, and activation of the three choices in *Choosing Purposeful Alignment*. With those choices, you elevate to the next level of the messy middle. In this elevated space, you are called forward into a stance that must be forward facing and directionally balanced to move you into a position of core strength. This type of game-changer posture enables you to bring all your layers into every situation, to trust your superpowers, to hold both joy and impact in your work, and to get comfortable with proximity to disequilibrium. All this allows you to lead with the most innovative, impactful, and significant strategies and ideas that are part of your work.

I shared with Ryan that this new stance creates greater clarity, humility, and gratitude. It unveils a profound ability to build deeper, more authentic connections. It makes a way for you to trust yourself to resist relationships, spaces, and situations that use your labor in a manner not aligned with your purpose. This slight shift from choosing to embodying is critical. It fuels readiness, motivation, and clarity regarding the *enabling conditions* and strategic action necessary to courageously ReSET your story. A powerful transformation occurs. Your evolved story emerges as the door shuts and the gap closes on the existing narrative you've been holding on to. With this necessary precursor to the embodiment of purposeful alignment, it's time to amplify your purpose.

As Ryan listened, his breathing grew heavier in this crucial moment. Resisting the urge to create comfort, I reminded him that choosing purposeful alignment is designed as a proposition to emerging, seasoned, and new game changers.

These changemakers and leaders are willing to be courageous and ask essential questions like the following:

- What could be possible if I explored the three choice points— The Power of Permission, Leaning into Transformation, and Become a Game Changer—as I travel through the messy middle of transformation?

- What greater impact could I have with the knowledge, power, and agency to choose purposeful alignment?

- How could this impact play out if I assumed this new stance without trepidation, and instead chose to move boldly, audaciously, and unapologetically?

Visionaries like my friend (and you) need to understand choosing is the critical first step in a cyclical and lifelong intention.

As I paused to allow space in my response, Ryan's breath quivered. Then came the question: "What is the game?"

I said, "The game is any story, complex issue, system, lever, circumstance, relationship, or space that must be innovated, interrupted, evolved, dismantled, or configured in service to deep impact and transformational change. To even begin to experience this necessary transformation, you must first choose purposeful alignment, then adjust your stance, and then embody your posture as a game changer. This is the process."

After a long pause, he gathered himself and asked five important questions:

1. How do I put this into practice in my life every day?
2. How do I shift from *choosing* to *becoming* a game changer to *embodying* being a game changer?
3. When will I know I've changed the game?
4. What is required to ReSET my story so I fully embody purposeful alignment and stand in it in a powerful way as a tool in every step, elevation, strategic decision, and space?
5. What's the path forward to get me there?

These five powerful questions are catalytic in crafting this next leg of the journey toward purposeful alignment. This is an elevated call to action and calling forward for all new, emerging, and seasoned leaders who accepted the proposition of choosing purposeful alignment. The Embodiment Journey can propel you forward in such a powerful way that your posture and stance move beyond the proposition to the full embodiment of the intentional ReSET of your story, a necessary requirement for changing the game.

> A game changer is an individual who drives transformational change.

The Invitation

When you reset your story, you are positioned differently and you are able to reset your life. You can't reset your life without resetting your story.

The ReSET Journey is intentionally designed to help you grapple with your Now Story and align it with the new story congruent with this powerful inflection point where you intentionally move from "choosing" to "embodiment." This journey is an invitation to interrogate your story and the accompanying narrative, so you can fully understand it and become familiar with your unique archetypes—the layers of who you are—that have been shared over time. This moves you toward clarity regarding your purpose and your why, while rewriting and embracing your new story as an important shift to the embodiment of purposeful alignment. Once you know your story, you can embrace being the author of it.

The ReSET is a continuous process that invites you into another level of the messy middle, a layered and cyclical transformational space constantly working to move you toward the embodiment of purposeful alignment.

The Messy Middle Is Layered and Cyclical

The messy middle, as a result of its cyclical nature, is constantly working to move you toward the embodiment of purposeful alignment.

The messy middle is the space between where you currently are and where you desire to be. It's multi-layered and cyclical. Each layer exposes new understanding, fear, opportunity, and resistance. These layers offer endless possibilities to reposition yourself for new areas of awareness, strategic choices, and transformation.

The messy middle is the space where the painful, often-unspoken work takes place, the work you whisper about to your most trusted comrades. Through this sacred work—which we often do not prioritize—we can achieve greater impact and work-life integration and move from success to significance. In this space, the ability to successfully navigate challenges and stand steadily requires asking hard questions.

The messy middle summons the necessity to ask yourself some powerful and often uncomfortable questions. It summons a state of vulnerability, where you drop down into a deeply feeling place and explore your conscious and unconscious emotions and how they show up in your body. It's a place that evokes active listening for yourself and observing what others say and reflect back to you. This state begs a high level of patience with yourself as you ease through both the external and internal noticing that comes with creating transparency and truth-telling about what you really desire. Here, you welcome a steady urgency that allows for just enough tension to stay the course on the journey toward purpose, while resisting complacency or paralysis. As you model compassionate leadership, you move through new and uncharted waters.

The messy middle is the place where game changers learn to embrace the necessary transformation that occurs at the "I" level in order to be a leader of organizations, strategic initiatives, and movements working on the cutting edge to drive complex social and transformational change. This space can reveal a variety of pain points and moments where the truth hurts and new awareness raises questions and uneasiness. Concurrently, in this space you might find a spark of new solutions and the revealing blind spots that enable you to name new challenges and opportunities for innovation. Here, disorientation, fear, discomfort, and uncertainty are heightened. In this place, you feel both powerful and powerless. Surviving and thriving in the messy middle requires you to ask questions such as "What if?" "What could be possible if?" and "What work do I need to do?" These critical questions lead to the creation of new narratives—your story— which require the interruption of your Now Story. As you make this shift, you're challenged to release long-held beliefs and actions, adopt new personal practices, and move forward in unapologetic truth-telling toward transformation.

Transitioning through the messy middle forces game changers to examine and interrogate purpose, alignment, values, and critical choice points while embracing an elevated posture. In the process, you might find yourself in a moment you can't quite articulate, and yet you recognize it as a critical inflection point you must boldly face and reimagine. You begin to recognize critical moments that call you into a role as a positive disruptor. By saying yes to what's possible, you move purposeful alignment from the fringes of your life to the center, as a non-negotiable.

So what is a game changer? A game changer is an individual who drives transformational change. And what is transformational change? It's the type of change that drives long-term impact and is void of transactional and performative activities meant to create the illusion of strategy and change. Game-changer status requires intentional space to address the hard questions of alignment and impact and the juxtaposition of your unique gifts and talents against an often complex environment or backdrop. So as you move into what it means to embody a game-changer posture, you must remember, again, what it means to become a game changer.

I first introduced the idea of becoming a game changer as a critical component to choosing purposeful alignment. Game changers are new, emerging, and seasoned leaders driving some of the most innovative work to address complex social change.

Game changers understand four critical principles:

1. Activate resources. It's imperative to activate every resource at your disposal to have greater impact and drive transformational change and impact.

2. Evolve continuously. You must constantly evolve, do the work, and anchor yourself deeply in your values and align them with every action.

3. Choose purposeful alignment. You choose to be purposefully aligned in every space, relationship, institution, and initiative as a non-negotiable.

4. Embrace the messy middle. You understand getting proximal and dropping down into the messy middle—the space between where you are and where you desire to be—is critical.

Game changers move from a place of stretching—moving past a perceived limit—to position themselves into a place where they choose to reset toward purposeful alignment. Your ability to stretch and be broken open in this posture and process enables you to continue to call yourself and others forward as you navigate the messy middle in this new embodiment posture and stance. In doing so, you begin to understand doing this work requires you to get comfortable in the disequilibrium, an essential part of the journey as you change the game. That disequilibrium is real and relevant to you fully stretching into the necessary work.

At this point, you may be wondering what disequilibrium is. I like to describe disequilibrium as the feeling of being off balance. It's a necessary part of the journey and is required to raise your commitment to change. As you embrace change and evolve, you unlearn old habits while building new skills to raise your emotional stamina. As your state of disequilibrium decreases and stamina increases, you're able to hold a higher vibration during change. In this new state, you easily choose to pivot through an intentional process. You become more aware of when you're operating at a lower vibration. This noticing allows you to quickly move to the highest emotional state that facilitates amplification of your skills and superpowers. In this higher state you're focused and motivated to maintain this dynamic energy. All this is necessary to drive transformation in your life, your community, your work, the complex issues you face, and the institutions you choose to serve.

When facing disequilibrium, you shift from seeing yourself as a participant in this journey toward purposeful alignment to viewing yourself as the tool that changes the game. The very moment you accept and embrace this truth, you walk into a new awareness of self. You begin to explore what is possible and experience a type of leveling up in your personal and professional life that's evident and catalytic in every space, relationship, story, complex issue, and institution. In this knowing without pause, you set intentions and model the practice for others. In this knowing, you clear the way for centering courageous conversations. You raise your vibration and flow, while modeling a new normal for others to emulate.

The process begins again as you continue to elevate while journeying through the messy middle. It becomes a cyclical journey, normalized in your work as a leader and change agent. With each cycle, you choose the journey that moves you closer to embodiment. With each practice, you resist holding your breath while waiting for the next cycle. Instead, you embrace it and integrate it into your entire being. As you sit with what's possible while moving through each cycle of the messy middle, a clear knowing—a new realization—washes over you. The messy middle, as a result of its cyclical nature, constantly works to move you toward the embodiment of purposeful alignment. But there's a step you can't skip: You have to ReSET your story in each cycle as you do the work toward purposeful alignment.

When you surrender to the journey, The ReSET normalizes the continuous process that gives you permission to realign and interrupt patterns in your stories. You learn to activate a different type of positioning and unleash new visions, dreams, desires, and purposeful alignment for your life.

In this space, you know these things to be true about The ReSET:

- When you shift your thinking, it shifts your feelings and, ultimately, your actions.

- You are constantly resetting. The narratives that worked for you last year may not work today.

- Every life change requires a reset in your story.

- You may try to change your life in ways incongruent with your vision for the future, inadvertently living out the same narrative over and over in response to an old story.

- When you ReSET your story, you reset your life. You can't ReSET your life without resetting your story.

- Activating yourself as a powerful tool to change the game and embody purposeful alignment in a fluid way becomes your natural flow.

- Knowing, owning, and telling your story is critical.

This understanding of what could be possible through embracing the ReSET practices enables you to release the old narrative about yourself that no longer serves you. It clears the way to shape new narratives about yourself, create new boundaries, gain clarity about what's healthy and what's toxic, and amplify your voice. By moving through this space, you ultimately shift the mental models that dictate your actions toward embodying a game-changer stance and staying on purpose.

Calling Forward and Setting Intentions

Choosing is not enough. You have to call forward to evoke embodiment.

The ReSET is a critical part of the journey that moves you from choosing to embodiment. In the first book, Choosing Purposeful Alignment, we focused on the proposition of what could be possible if you chose to align your purpose. Throughout the chapters, you were invited to choose permission and transformation and to explore what it would mean to become a game changer. These powerful choices were designed to explore what could be possible and to create a clear line of sight. However, that work didn't fully prepare you to embody and practice purposeful alignment in every part of your life, every day.

This next phase, The ReSET Journey, builds upon those choices. This explicit and necessary invitation of calling forward jolts you into a movement that propels you into an embodied game-changer posture. In this embodied posture, it's clear to you and visible to others that you are walking in your purpose and holding a game-changer stance.

On the Zoom call with amazing leaders from across the world grappling with what it means to be a leader in this moment, I was struck by the wealth of information shared. New concepts, ideas, and perspectives percolated in the space and challenged me in new ways. I paused at critical moments to let the meaty conversations wash over me. At times, I needed to turn off my camera so I could fully process the depths of the offerings in the space. As I sat there, off camera, looking out the window, I closed my eyes to reconcile the cognitive dissonance I was moving through. I found myself in the conversation that made the distinction between calling out, calling in, and calling forward. This calling forward evoked such a powerful image for me, one of failing forward. Yes, examining the lessons learned from missing the mark, but most importantly, doing the intentional work to resist being paralyzed by failure.

When we see everything as valuable information, we accept the necessity to persist through it, and we gain the powerful momentum to connect to other ideas, people, movements, and initiatives.

Calling forward is an invitation to take a deeper dive into embodiment and consequently The ReSET Journey. As Justin Michael Williams and Shelly Tygielski so eloquently explain in their 2024 article in *Nonprofit Quarterly*, "Calling People Forward Instead of Out: Ten Essential Steps," calling forward is an invitation to be something greater. While out/in is fighting against what we hate, calling forward is building upon what we love. Calling forward invites people into a greater state of integration and evolution, and opens the door to real transformation. The outcome, although not always immediate, is often surprising. The authors go on to say that you can call anyone forward, but it doesn't mean they're going to immediately walk toward you; it's a journey.[1]

---

[1] Justin Michael Williams and Shelly Tygielski, "Calling People Forward Instead of Out: Ten Essential Steps," Nonprofit Quarterly, March 4, 2024, https://nonprofitquarterly.org/calling-people-forward-instead-of-out-ten-essential-steps/

The ReSET is an invitation to call you forward in an incremental way, into a journey that unleashes greatness and greater impact. The calling forward process is meant for you to consciously work at a higher vibration, vantage point and posture to unleash unimaginable impact across each component of your life and walk. This calling forward invitation is for new, emerging, and seasoned game changers that desire to join The ReSET Journey.

The ReSET Journey requires an elevated discipline that calls you forward into three critical components: pausing, pivoting, and assuming a powerful Forward Stance. Throughout the process, you are called to embrace an emergent approach focused on testing, doing, and learning. This approach allows you to unlearn and relearn along the way, to view The ReSET as a seamless part of your practice of tackling the complexity that comes with transformational change. Throughout the ReSET process, you are called forward over and over again to create and cultivate the right thinking, enabling conditions, emotions, and vibrations needed to re-write your stories. This process requires you to master a framework that includes five core practices:

1. R-Realize
2. E-Engage
3. S-Self-Authenticate
4. E-Establish
5. T- Talk About It

By leaning into a calling-forward posture, you're invited to first create powerful intentions as you prepare for The ReSET Journey. Intention setting is a practice of consciously choosing how you want to be, feel, or engage in the world. Write these intentions in a journal or place them in a highly visible place to keep you accountable on this journey. The preparation process invites you to embrace powerful thinking grounded in what could be possible, thinking that allows you to color outside of the traditional lines and imagine bigger than ever. This interrupts self-limiting beliefs that dim your new story by leaving any possibilities on the table that should be considered or incorporated.

As with any new posture, you will be required to stretch beyond what's comfortable. Don't cower or avoid this. This new elevated discipline is taking you to new heights, and you're ready for it. Be open to seeing the truth within the fears and mini stories that reveal themselves as you give yourself permission to lean into this experience. This is part of your growth. As you unlearn and relearn, you become, evolve, and embody who you were destined to be. Be open to tapping into the love, guidance, and strength of the people in your circle of influence. You will need their support to carry you through.

And so The ReSET begins.

CHAPTER 2

THE RESET JOURNEY BEGINS: AN ELEVATED DISCIPLINE

I felt unprepared to navigate, but I knew in every fiber of my being that I had to meet the moment.

An elevated discipline calls you forward to actively demonstrate a high degree of self-control. In addition, you establish the ability to consistently act in alignment with your purpose, goals, and values in the face of distractions, temptations, or having to make a stand as a game changer. It's about more than just willpower; it involves developing habits, routines, and a mindset that support focused action and long-term achievement. As you sustain these new positions over time, you're poised to meet each moment with focus and courage.

Meeting the Moment

As usual, I arrived at the meeting early to set up the space in our favorite U-shaped configuration. I loved getting there early to ensure everyone felt the intentionality of the space—music playing, snacks laid out, and slides on the screen—so I could be present when each person arrived. This ritual had become increasingly important as the group energy had shifted, signaling a new era of our collective work. We seemed to be operating at a lower vibration, which resulted in unspoken conflicts.

This tension required more space and patience to move through mis-understandings so we could gain alignment in our collective work.

Over a year, I'd noticed individuals had stopped doing their requisite "I" work before communing in this sacred space. That deep "I" work was necessary to tackle complex issues, model the way, and hold resistance to the systems we desired to interrupt. The "I" work, refers to the deep internal work that allows you to show up positive and self-aware, to resist harming others in the midst of difficult moments, and to make healthy choices to meet others in the work. Only with this necessary personal work complete could each person show up healthy, connected, and focused on the collective agenda and effectively champion our work. This was a moment of growth and reimagining, a moment when I needed to see everything as information so I could receive the lessons and the medicine needed to grow forward.

On this particular day, the energy was thick and quite a bit of it undoubtedly channeled toward me. This wasn't new; it had become a pattern over the years. This year, however, it had come to an inflection point.

As I focused on the layers of what each person was communicating, I felt my mother's hand on my leg (out of the view of others). She had been a part of this collective work from the very beginning. Her touch silently reminded me to breathe, which I did. I asked authentic and curious questions, leaned in to demonstrate my interest and engagement, asked permission to share what I heard, and listened for next steps as we moved the conversation to consensus. As everyone exited the room at the conclusion of the meeting, I sat silently, in deep consideration of what had just unfolded.

These questions circled in my mind as I worked to make some meaning of it all:

- What is unspoken here? What's the question underneath the question?
- What do they need me to hear?

- What do they want to change as a result of them showing up in this way?

- What are they expecting or desiring from this exchange?

- Who hurt them?

- What permissions have they received from this space to show up in a toxic and harmful way and without a clear line of sight toward naming solutions, resolutions, repair, or reconciliation?

As the room cleared, I returned it to its previous state, moving quietly and wrestling with the questions in my head. When I finally let out a huge sigh, those who remained in the space took notice and wanted to intercede.

"How can we support you, Tracey?" they asked.

I closed my eyes in contemplation before speaking. "Honestly, this entire experience is causing me to negotiate within myself," I said. The truth was I needed to determine when to put my coach hat on and when to create boundaries with certain individuals I never thought I'd have to segment at that level. I silently acknowledged I was in the messy middle again, this time, at an elevated level that invited me into a new part of my story. This new space was uncomfortable and caused me to fumble through it.

In the midst of finding my emotional footing, I found myself negotiating at the intersection of being paralyzed, noticing, and staying at the high vibration of my emotional ladder. In this new stage of the messy middle, I understood the cost and results of not meeting this moment: me being disoriented and distracted, limiting my impact on this deep transformational work, and not sustaining my overall well-being and joy. I also began to see clues about how things would have to shift in this new cycle and at each stage of the messy middle. New choices would be necessary as I worked to make a more complete story in this space. Things would shift for me going forward, not from a place of pain, grief, or sadness, but from a place of understanding my embodiment journey of purposeful alignment was inviting me to move differently.

Although I had journeyed through the process of choosing purposeful alignment, I realized I hadn't been fully practicing it to unleash everything possible. The universe had amplified what I had been resisting and refused to acknowledge in this faith walk. I knew innately in that moment that this stage of the experience was different and would require me to embody it. I had moved into another cycle and an elevated level of the messy middle that I felt unprepared to navigate. The messy middle had created the necessary conditions to shift critical mindsets, adjust my stance and posture, understand my Now Story, and ready me to reset my story toward the embodiment of purposeful alignment.

All this required me to move into an elevated discipline I'd never experienced, but which I knew in every fiber of my being I had to meet in the moment. An unspoken desire and a new story that needed to emerge were collectively seeking further alignment. It was time for a course correction to ensure alignment with my embodied purpose and game-changer posture.

An Elevated Discipline: The Pause, The Pivot, and Forward Stance

And so The ReSET begins. It begins with the understanding that an elevated discipline is required, a type of discipline where you continuously work at something that is or is perceived to be difficult. This elevated discipline constantly and continuously calls you forward to navigate, persist through, and move to the next level of embodiment by embracing, normalizing, and practicing three distinct disciplines.

Discipline 1—The Pause: There's power in The Pause. This type of discipline invites you to just wait for it. The "it" could be a variety of things, such as information, synergy, visible patterns, or the resolution of a complex issue that sets the stage for new opportunities. This type of discipline requires you to resist quick reactions in response to new information, discoveries, situations, discomfort, change, or feelings of disequilibrium. With The Pause, you ready yourself to pivot in just the right direction and moment.

Discipline 2—The Pivot: Making the slightest adjustment or shift to gain a better perspective enables you to make a more complete story and identify multiple paths of possibility moving forward. This type of discipline is strategic. It sees everything as information that provides clues to enable you to course correct and strategically realign.

Discipline 3—Forward Stance: After pausing and then pivoting, you're ready to move into an elevated posture of a Forward Stance that can be sustained and heightened over time. Forward Stance requires you to move from an elevated position as an embodied game changer to a position where you actively and consistently align with your clear purpose and you own the authorship of your new story. This type of discipline builds core muscles, stretches you, and enables you to approach anything from a place of strength and power. It allows you to sustain and hold an elevated posture and eventually move to another level of heightened impact. By adjusting your posture to one where you naturally operate out of your strength and clear purpose, you seamlessly move to Forward Stance, which is the final and most critical part of The ReSET.

Think of an instance when you had to meet the moment.

- What were you required to name and notice?

____

____

- Which elevated discipline do you wish you had embraced: The Pause, The Pivot, or a Forward Stance?

____

____

Practice and Accountability

Developing an elevated discipline does not happen on its own; it requires intentional practice, and accountability. This practice doesn't focus on perfection. Instead, it requires a heightened capacity to be intentional in every decision, discussion, action, and engagement. Practice allows you to build muscles that enable clarity in your perception of challenging versus hard. Practice allows for opportunities to meet each moment of the work you consented to do through The ReSET Journey.

As you practice, you stretch into a state of becoming an intentional architect of your journey toward embodiment. Practice is an invitation to experiment. Here, you set the stage for mini experiences. You test, do, and learn processes that create space for radical imagination, innovation, and uncharted pathways. As you lean in and meet this moment, you experience a powerful journey that moves you toward the embodiment of your purpose. This visible movement demonstrates steadiness in the face of discomfort.

With practice, what you perceived as hard is redefined as challenging. In this discipline, you model what it looks like to lean into curiosity. You become compelled to ask powerful questions in the face of difficult scenarios and relationships. Along the way, you learn to view everything as information, and you resist and suspend the urge to withdraw from powerful moments that can stretch you beyond your perceived limits.

As your discipline strengthens, you're compelled to stay the course until just the right moment, when you're on the cusp of a breakthrough or clarity. Ultimately, you're prepared to anchor yourself in a normalized cadence, a natural state of awareness, permission, choice, and strategic action. All this is necessary to realign and interrupt patterns that create barriers to true embodiment of your purpose.

Each cadence and rhythm offers crescendos. A new normal and critical practice prepares you for the next cycle, where you meet each moment and layer of the messy middle of transformation. In these moments, you learn to give yourself permission to adjust patterns in your stories. You do this by activating a different type of positioning. You unleash new thinking and visions. You level up your leadership. You activate strategic action aligned with your purpose.

Although your practice as an individual is a critical part of the formula, practicing with an accountability circle amplifies the Embodiment Journey. An accountability circle provides a unique opportunity to walk with others willing to celebrate you, ask you difficult questions, and push your thinking, all while they embark on the same journey. This unity is priceless. The ability to hold each other accountable leads you to become responsible for your actions and the results of those choices.

Accountability is not meant to be punitive. It's a signal of solidarity and support. It creates the space to sharpen each other as leaders and game changers as you all commit to the same preparation and practice in your everyday walk. This walk is not meant to be traveled alone. It is designed to build a movement that creates a critical groundswell of innovation, leadership, and impact across our professional and personal lives.

As you begin your ReSET Journey, answer the following questions:

- In what ways will you create space to practice in order to move through The ReSET Journey?

____

____

- What could enable success and help you to achieve your goals? What could get in the way?

____

____

- What circle of accountability will you put in place to ensure you move through each discipline of the journey?

  ____

  ____

- What are you most excited about?

  ____

  ____

ELEVATED DISCIPLINE 1:

THE POWER OF THE PAUSE

I'm a big basketball fan and grew up playing the sport. After school, I'd rush home to get on the basketball courts, which were often busy, colorful, and full of energy with full-court games dominated by local players and teams. My passion for basketball continued through middle and high school as I worked hard to secure my position as a shooting guard on our school's basketball team.

Not everyone loved basketball as much as I did, so some of those who didn't asked me, "What do you love about the game?"

My reply: "I love the energy of the game, the crowd, and the competitiveness. But most of all, I love the feel of the ball as I turn it over and over in my hands."

The combination of the smoothness of the leather and the deep ridges in the basketball, as it slid across my palms and fingers with each dribble, created a tactile sensation that anchored me to take what I always hoped would be the perfect shot from any corner of the court. I'd intentionally reposition myself away from the crowd of players who pushed against each other underneath the basketball goal. From a distance, I had enough space to pause and view the players. Then, I would wait for just the right angle and timing to take the optimal shot.

There's power in The Pause. That momentary halt allows for preparation and awareness to move you toward an embodied purpose. But don't confuse The Pause with a hard stop. Stopping suggests your effort, creativity, and ability have come to an end. Instead, The Pause is an invitation to reposition and sharpen your ability and focus. During The Pause you wait for the optimal moment that moves you closer to greater alignment and impact.

By embracing a posture of pausing, you create space for noticing and naming and for making strategic and intentional choices. This slight act drives you closer to new awareness, allows you to experiment, and reveals new opportunities, ideas, and partnerships. The process of radical pausing allows for muscle building. Here, your expertise is amplified, bringing you to an elevated discipline that resists immediate reactions.

The Pause brings space to ask powerful questions. It sharpens your curiosity and engages you to notice and trust the clues and trends that emerge just on the horizon. Through a more focused lens, you can spot the right position, move with grace, and welcome critical indicators that invite nimbleness, sharp pivots, and a Forward Stance.

Pausing is the first elevated discipline necessary to prepare you for the first phase of The ReSET Journey. It invites you to actively interrogate and interrupt long-held stories that distort what's possible and keep you from your embodied purpose. With The Pause, you shift your thinking and embrace a series of readiness practices that build your muscles as you shift your mindset, your realization, and your engagement.

ReSET Mindset: It's All About the Mental

The ReSET requires focused attention on your thinking, which consists of your mental models and mindsets. Mental models are created from the stories you have crafted and tell yourself. These mental models reveal your conscious and unconscious biases about an issue, individual, community, institution, situation, feeling, or relationship. They become a lens for how you see the world.

Developing new mental models invites new questions, curiosities, possibilities, fears, and opportunities all designed to realign and reset powerful narratives. As such, mental models lay the foundation to consciously shift your power, choices, and agency regarding where you'll use your labor to embody purposeful alignment.

The first time I was introduced to the inverted pyramid, I was blown away. It provided explicit language, multiple entry points, and understanding of the dimensions of deep change. That understanding now shapes the way I see the world.

A colleague had forwarded me a link as we created an intentional experience for an important staff retreat. I printed the article and read it over and over, studying the brightly colored diagram that simplified each of the six conditions of systems change: policies, practices, resource flows, relationships and connections, power dynamics, and mental models.[2] This moment gifted me a new level of clarity, a new tool, a practice, and a mindset that would become permanent in all aspects of my life.

I held the pages of the article in one hand and a highlighter in the other, moving from line to line, resisting any distractions and the impulse to skim. If I read too quickly, I feared I'd miss critical pieces needed to heighten my awareness and analysis. Finally, I pulled myself

---

[2] John Kania, Mark Kramer, and Peter Senge, "The Water of Systems Change," FSG, June 4, 2018, https://www.fsg.org/resource/water_of_systems_change/

away from the article to ponder its depth. In that moment, I mumbled a single question to myself: "How could a simple diagram create such a powerful framing to hold the complexity of systems change by identifying six critical conditions, emphasizing that the most powerful and transformational condition was shifting mental models?"

In response to my own question, I said, "It's all about the mental, the mindset. And ultimately, the mindset creates the necessary conditions to reset a powerful story and narrative."

The Power of the Narrative

A story is a sequence of events that occurs. A narrative focuses on how that story is told, shared, and revealed publicly to others. The narrative can be true or fictitious. Being aware of the truth of your narrative is an integral part of your transformational process. As a game changer, resetting both your story and the narrative is important. The juxtaposition of what emerges as truth and fiction from grappling with both can be a recipe for a powerful story. That story either propels you forward with energy, imagination, and vision, or it keeps you confined to self-limiting beliefs and inaction.

The first phase of The ReSET focuses on shifting your mental models and your mindset in response to this awareness. You've heard stories about yourself that may hold some truth, but may also contain some false information. You've heard them so many times that you begin to retell them, eventually becoming complicit in keeping that narrative in place, despite an emerging counter-story. The new story slowly reveals all the unconscious bias, powerful truths and falsehoods, and key elements of your origin story.

Shifting mental models is one of the most powerful ways to activate and take agency of your individual and collective power. In doing so, you shift where you use your labor and capital; negotiate new networks, proximity, and access in your relationships; and normalize healthy practices that serve to embodying purposeful alignment. Ultimately your mindset creates the necessary conditions to reset a powerful narrative.

Your mindset is comprised of deeply held beliefs that shape how you process who you are and how you fit in the world around you. Your mindset is a critical lever that influences how you think, feel, and act in any given situation. What you think influences how you feel, and your feelings impact your choices and actions. Therefore, your mindset relates to your ability to achieve your goals and, ultimately, your success. Further, your mindset—in particular a growth mindset—allows you to see challenges not as insurmountable, but as opportunities for growth, discovery, and evolution. Consequently, this growth mindset becomes an antidote to a fixed mindset, which views challenging situations as impossible and rewards compliance and comfort.

Psychologist Carol Dweck, PhD, identified five characteristics of a growth mindset: embracing learning, working hard, welcoming challenges, taking feedback constructively, and failing forward.[3] These traits serve as the foundation to reset your story and the overall narrative, supporting your ongoing work to adjust and evolve your mindset. These characteristics help position you and support your new posture and game-changer stance toward the embodiment of purposeful alignment.

When your mindset is out of alignment with your story, you move toward a more fixed or limited mindset, and you become more susceptible to disempowering beliefs that may fuel false stories about your preparedness. Your ability to embrace a mindset focused on growth and stretching and setting in place the right conditions for success is key to this elevated discipline of pausing, pivoting, and Forward Stance. Your elevated mindset moves you into a place where your awareness is sharpened, allowing you to distinguish what is true, what is fear, what is medicine, and what is false. With that, you're armed with new muscles to pivot and adjust your posture.

---

[3] "Carol Dweck: A Summary of Growth and Fixed Mindsets," fs.com, https://fs.blog/carol-dweck-mindset/

Answer the following questions to understand your mindset and how you can adjust it to support your ReSET Journey:

- What new mindset will you need on this leg of your journey?

____

____

- Is your current mindset one of growth, or is it fixed?

____

____

- What powerful beliefs do you need to embrace to create a new story and narrative?

____

____

- What disempowering beliefs should you confront and release to create a new story and narrative?

____

____

- Considering all five characteristics of a growth mindset, where are your growing edges?

____

____

- What is your next best step toward embracing a mindset that enables you to lean into The ReSET Journey?

____

____

- What tools do you need to guide you through the ReSET process?

____

____

Let's move into the first practice of The ReSET Journey, Realize.

CHAPTER 3

R—REALIZE

*What new realizations, thinking, and deep beliefs are necessary for
you to move into an elevated posture of embodiment to embrace this
new and elevated story of yourself?*

Realization is the act of becoming fully aware of something as fact.
As the first practice in The ReSET Journey, Realization focuses
on strategically adjusting the lens through which you view the world,
a view that ultimately influences your mindset, beliefs, and thinking
throughout your ReSET Journey.

The practice of Realization is foundational and creates the readiness
for subsequent steps. In those ensuing stages, you name, interrogate,
and acknowledge the mindset critical to propel you forward. In this
ReSET Journey toward your aligned future story, you move from a
choice to be purposefully aligned to choose critical noes and yeses that
propel you toward embodying your purpose.

To ReSET your narrative requires you to realize your current story
and all the mini stories within it are out of alignment. In essence, you
evolve from a place of making critical choices from an antiquated
story that does not serve you. Remaining in this place would keep you
from embodying an elevated posture. In this moment of Realization,
you become aware of yourself and your purpose, thereby bringing
your impact into alignment with the direction in which you're headed.

It's critical and necessary to create a new story, one aligned with what's next and which arms you with the practices and tools needed for today and every future moment as a game changer.

This lens invites you to view yourself in three distinct ways as you shift from choosing to embodiment.

1. First, you have to deeply believe in and see yourself as the instrument with agency and permission to make a more complete and truer story about your purpose and posture as a game changer.

2. Next, this evolved lens moves you strategically into a position to accept that you are the author of your story.

3. Lastly, this thinking allows you to view the explicit choices you have to make as a gifting of critical information. At this point, you become a truth teller on your own path forward. You embrace a new and more accurate way of seeing yourself, and you accept disruption as the necessary medicine to create the motivation and comfort to ReSET your story.

By using this different lens, you begin the process of adjusting your mindset and thinking in a way that strategically positions you for success on this journey.

ReSET Mindset 1: You Are the Instrument

What could be possible if you saw yourself as your own instrument?

I've had the privilege of learning from Damian and Jermaine Johnson, the founders of No Grease, Inc., and countless other barber entrepreneurs about the sacredness of the barbershop. In this place, energy is important, connection and relationship are critical, and confidentiality is vital. In the barbershop, courageous conversations are had, truth telling occurs, healing and support are provided, and vulnerability is displayed. In this sacred space, advice from lived experience is shared, considered, and affirmed, leaving a buzz of energy and shared understanding that reaches far beyond the walls of the barbershop to the world at large.

I had wrestled with a deeper understanding about the uniqueness of this space for weeks as I watched a talented young entrepreneur barber struggle to connect with his clients. His technique was amazing, but so much of barbering is relational. I could see the strain in his body language as he labored to connect with and even touch his clients in a way that didn't feel awkward or forced. Something held him back, and I wondered what would drive someone who was uncomfortable with touching others and being in connection with diverse clientele to choose a profession that requires connection, relationship, and constantly touching people.

On one occasion, he finished a service and removed the protective cape from his client. Then, he walked the client to the register to close out the appointment. As I observed, these questions lingered in my mind: What's getting in the way of this connection? What discomfort is he feeling? What's its origin? What does he need to fully operate in his greatness? What if he could see what could be possible? What if he could see himself as his own instrument? Ultimately, he transitioned from the industry and decided to focus on his music full-time, delaying the opportunity to grapple with these questions.

Shifting from choosing to becoming a game changer and then to an embodiment posture of a game-changer stance requires you to see yourself as your own instrument. This intentional shift serves as an invitation to envision yourself as a unique tool, razor sharp, leading and working on the cutting edge of innovation, professionally and personally. You assume a stance that shifts from an antiquated approach, focused on having power over individuals, initiatives, and spaces, to one explicitly about sharing, building, wielding, and transferring power together. Consequently, you create conditions to walk alongside others rather than in front of them. In this posture, you commit to sharpening others and yourself. All the while, you thrive as a constant learner committed to being an expert and a master of your craft and your role.

When you deeply believe you're the instrument that can change the game, you stand in your agency as the author of your own story. Even if you haven't written it yet, this new story is more aligned with your clear line of sight, a new vision of your why, your purpose, and your calling in the world.

ReSET Mindset 2: Authoring Your Own Story

You are the instrument in charge of authoring your story. Being unwavering in this stance, knowledge, and commitment is a non-negotiable.

In this practice of Realization, you must come to the deep understanding and truth that you are the instrument and, therefore, the primary author of your own story of what's possible. As the author, you have the ability to make key decisions regarding your story. Here, you learn to resist embracing the false stories of others. You explore and then reveal all your layers, which hold multiple truths of who you are. Consequently, you heighten your new authentic story while lowering the volume on and dismissing the stories created by people operating from a hidden agenda or low vibration.

As I prepared for my long drive home, I paused to reflect on the day-long retreat. There had been some powerful moments when I stepped back during each conversation that unfolded and just observed, not only the group, but also myself. I noted when my awareness was heightened and when I finally gave myself permission to both see and believe the truth. I reflected on the moment my breathing slowed as I listened to one of the participants repeat the words I had spoken countless times in my life's work. They flowed from her tongue as if she was their author, attempting to take credit and gain credibility in this shared space. Each word became more pronounced, drowning out the chatter in the room. And there it was—the clearing, the quiet moment. I saw the truth that she was scared, that she didn't know who she was, and that she had pulled together pieces of others' stories and personalities to craft a story for herself.

In that moment, I paused so I could notice, name, and release parts of my Now Story that did not serve me. I accepted that no matter what type of support I had provided, no matter how much grace I gave, no matter how much relational and social capital I extended, no matter how much strategic thought partnership and walking in solidarity with her I invested, she was comfortable working at a low vibration. She was only interested in crafting a limited story of who I was to deflect from her own discomfort of self. She opted to ignore her own unmet desires. She chose to deflect from her limited perspective and story about herself, not realizing the story would always be present.

This participant was deeply invested in a limited and false story about me that served her, and she was unwilling to release it due to her fear. In that moment, I knew the truth: The tension constantly in the air was my resistance to her story and my unwillingness to be complicit in her story about me. The opinions of others, including hers, would always be there. It was my responsibility to be the author of my story, turn down the volume, and be unbothered by their discomfort and fear around the power of my story. I was the instrument in charge of authoring my story, and I was unwavering in this stance. Knowledge and commitment were non-negotiables.

As I realized then, creating an aligned narrative allows the unfolding of your layers, and can reveal the following:

- Who you truly are. You realize a significant level of comfort in the face of the discomfort of others. In the spaces you choose to occupy and engage, you no longer wait for others to affirm or commit to this new way of being, your new story.

- Your clarity and boldness. These elements serve as preparation for action and deep belief that you can navigate the impact, consequences, and ripples that emerge from your strategic decisions. You stand boldly in your voice, gifts, passion, and power.

- Your clearly stated yeses and noes. For every yes you make along this journey, you're required to intentionally make three noes. With each choice, the gap between uncertainty and your strategic choices is diminished, allowing you to take critical steps.

- A normalized way of being. Practices that indicate you have done the work to ReSET become embedded in your being. You have demonstrated your ability to manage the messy middle. You have now embodied and revealed your story and adjusted your stance with each opportunity to embody a game-changer posture.

- A clearer understanding of what is true and not true. You now trust yourself in a new way. You move through necessary repair based on what's revealed.

- Your understanding that the work is continuous. The journey continues from here. You maintain the posture of embodying a game changer. You stand ready and willing to do what's necessary at each opportunity, professionally and personally, toward purposeful alignment.

ReSET Mindset 3: The Power to Choose + Choice Points

You have the ability to choose, and there is power in choosing, particularly when you understand you are the instrument.

Choice points are different than choices. A choice is one option among many. Choice points, however, are powerful and specific moments when you consciously choose a behavior that either aligns with your values, purpose, and focus, or leads you to act in a manner inconsistent with values, purpose, and focus.

Choice points require you to pause before acting, and they provide moments of intense personal and professional growth. When you choose to act in alignment with your values, these critical moments move you away from a mindset that fuels false narratives—where you embrace a powerless victim mentality and a belief that something is happening to you—and into a place of power to make small, incremental decisions that have a significant impact and cause a ripple of results in The ReSET Journey.

Embracing the power of small choices is a critical shift. When you recognize your choice points, you release yourself from limitations and accept small choices as an important shift to move you onto a different path. With this shift, you drive the direction of the outcome through your incremental choices. You arrive at the truth that you have the ability to choose and there is agency and power in choosing.

The act of choosing shifts you from a place of disorientation to one of clarity. Critical decision-making opportunities influence outcomes, and the cumulative impacts of small choices can be as significant as the impact of a single big decision. You move from a place of surviving to thriving and from a place of unbalanced to balanced. You move from hesitancy to explicitly naming, exploring, and imagining a series of first yeses at each interaction of the journey. When you know you're in purposeful alignment—a shift from success to significance to being transformational—you create the readiness and momentum to accept the invitation and the choice to arrive at a significant moment in your journey.

One of the more powerful moments I had as the concept of this ReSET Journey was revealed to me occurred when I spoke to Bank of America Women's Summit, an employee special-interest group at national BofA headquarters. While I was onstage, a woman asked a powerful question regarding a complicated but common family dynamic: "How do I deal with toxic family members I don't want to engage with on a regular basis?"

As she paused to take a breath after her intentional vulnerability, I met her gaze and replied, "No one is entitled to proximity and access to you."

The room buzzed with an audible "Oh, wow!" As she sat with that powerful notion, she asked for tools to support her in making the shift from allowing to choosing who comes into her circle.

"You are the instrument," I replied. "You have the power to choose to say yes or no to those relationships." Again, the room let out a huge sigh with an energy that engulfed the room like a choir singing in harmony.

This new thinking deepens the work of unlearning and interrupting messages and narratives you hold on to and those shared by others. Unhealthy and false thinking can be buried like a hidden secret in minds and hearts, and it becomes revealed as you travel to the next layer of the messy middle. The explicit practice of choosing and creating intentional choice points provides a way forward for building new muscles of naming and noticing. This serves as fuel to persist through the discomfort of learning new messages and narratives that position you as an instrument, adding another level of clarity on your journey. This practice was introduced in *Choosing Purposeful Alignment: The Messy Middle of Transformation* through the use of the Yes Map.

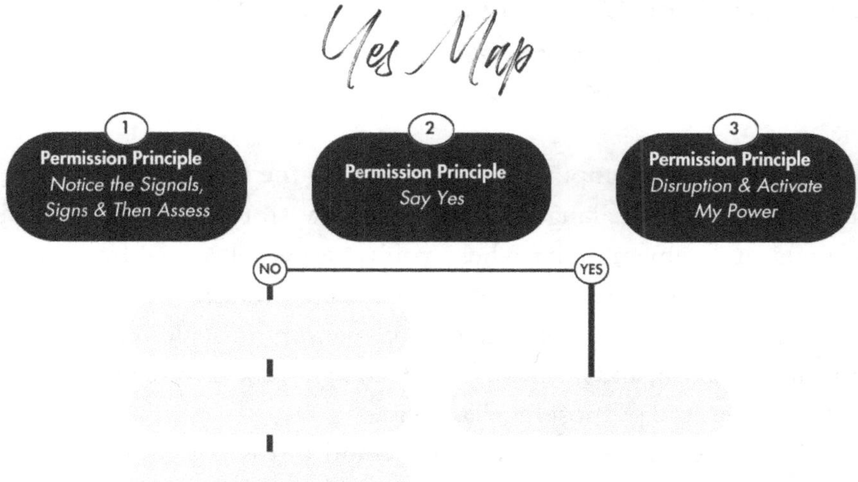

The Yes Map was designed to normalize the power of choosing, and to provide a tool to practice saying yes and no. The practice of choosing creates spaciousness to unearth and interrupt beliefs, practices, and fears that serve as barriers to your forward motion toward purposeful alignment. As you practice intentionally choosing, you demonstrate that you can seamlessly move into the driver's seat of your story as the author through the practice of intentional yeses and noes. This stance and way of thinking leads you to important intentions needed to move you to the next phase and layer of the messy middle. Three noes are required to make room for every yes, creating the practice, synergy, and readiness for the ripple effect of your unique purpose.

Inventory Your Choice Points, Yeses, and Noes

Give yourself permission to remember. Remembering is a powerful tool to create greater awareness of your journey toward purposeful alignment.

Remembering is an important step in owning the choices you've made and are currently making to shape your new story. There's power in naming and remembering where you've been. This enables you to declare where you desire to go and to keep your line of sight clear toward your purpose. Refreshing your memory provides clues, valuable information, and moments of greater awareness to further clarify your journey and purposeful alignment.

Remembering allows you to name and assess the conscious and unconscious choice points you create. As a result, you give yourself permission to practice being present and strategic in every choice you make. You must normalize and embody this practice in every aspect of your life as you define your story moving forward.

Remembering Inventory Exercise

Let's step back for a moment and inventory the work. Take some time to remember all the significant choices you made in the last three months. Inventory all your yeses and noes to affirm you're where you're supposed to be on this journey.

This inventory process is a critical first step as you ready yourself to normalize the new story of self and release the mini stories, those necessary patterns and pieces you have to notice and name. Those yeses and noes in your mini stories serve as important prompts to remind you that you have agency and power. They also alert you to stay in your body and acknowledge your thoughts, feelings, and actions, and they invite you to move to strategic activation, ultimately creating a firm foundation and a normalized way of being. This prepares you to reset a new, more truthful, and powerful story to propel you forward.

Let's inventory all your yeses and noes.

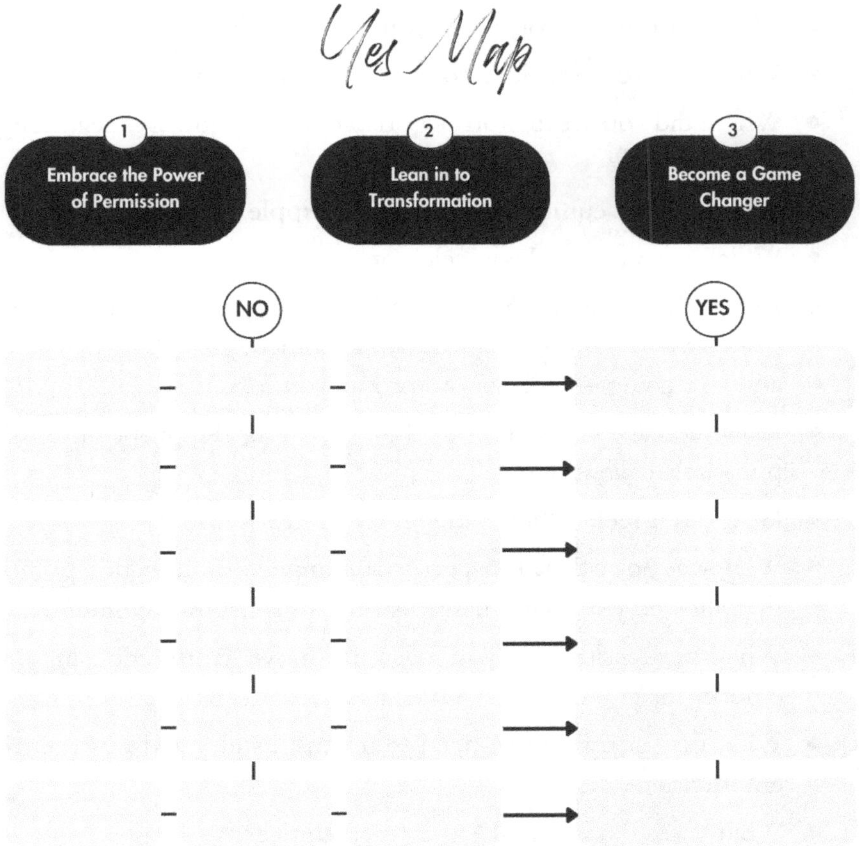

Given your experience of walking through or orienting yourself to the three choice points in the first phase of this journey—The Power of Permission, Leaning into Transformation, and Become a Game

Changer—and the clues revealed from your yes map, respond to the following:

- What patterns do you see in your three choices?
- Where did you prioritize your yeses in each choice?
- Where did you create non-negotiables and boundaries regarding your noes?
- What was the cumulative impact and ripple of your yeses?
- Which moments did you celebrate?
- In which moments did you embrace the growing edges—the places where your current capabilities meet growth, expansion, and stretching—necessary to propel you forward?
- How did each yes shift your thinking about the proposition of purposeful alignment?
- How did it feel? Where did you feel it in your body?
- What was one of the most profound impacts or inflection points that allowed you to ultimately choose purposeful alignment?
- What permission do you need to move from choosing to embodying?
- What new story do you need to tell in this elevated posture of embodiment?
- What yeses did you make after each choice?
- Which ones were you able to keep?
- What noes did you make after each choice?
- Which ones were you able to keep?
- What clues did each of these yeses and noes that you kept reveal to you about your purpose?

Given this new awareness and opportunity to inventory your choice points, answer the following:

- Where do you need to pause your story to increase your awareness and realization regarding these key concepts?

  ____

  ____

- How do you need to shift your thinking to fully embrace that you are the author of your story?

  ____

  ____

- What parts of your story do you need to reconcile as true or false to see yourself as an instrument with the power to make strategic choices to align with your embodied purpose?

  ____

  ____

- What disempowering beliefs and actions do you need to interrupt?

  ____

  ____

- What powerful beliefs and actions do you need to embrace?

  ____

  ____

- What best next choice are you intentionally making to move you closer to the embodiment of your purpose?

  ____

  ____

Embodied game changers accept that they are the author of their story *and* the tool. When you ReSET your story in a factual way, you unleash yourself and your choices boldly and unapologetically to change the game. You find that you are what people are seeking in their partnerships, collaborations, and work toward unleashing deep transformational impact.

CHAPTER 4

E—ENGAGE

*What conditions will prepare you to embrace this new and elevated
story? What thinking and feelings do you need to name, interrogate,
and move through toward an elevated posture of embodiment?*

Engage is the second practice in The ReSET Journey. It focuses on
preparation and what's required to hold your attention so you can
name, interrogate, and move toward an elevated posture of embodiment. Engage provides the space to explore and execute the necessary
conditions to successfully craft and embrace your evolved story.

*What enabling conditions are necessary to evoke a powerful movement
forward and shift you from choosing to embodiment of a game-changer posture?*
As I grappled with this question, a powerful memory surfaced of an
experience I had when a new type of disequilibrium jolted me in such
a significant way that it created a shift.

There I was, waiting to board a plane to work with my final client
partner of the year, when a voice on the phone informed me the work
for the following year had been paused. A sudden rush of images
emerged. Choice points appeared, and faces of potential client partners I hadn't committed to for the following year came rushing back

like a flash of lightning right before my eyes. It was the last month of the final quarter of the year, and there was no going back. Instead, I had to pause and surrender to what would happen next. I had to trust and believe deeply that I was prepared and had put in place the conditions necessary for success.

In the moment, I knew three important things:

1. I had to pause and not react. In The Pause, I could ask questions to gain additional information and insight.

2. Pausing, along with engaging, would allow me to listen more deeply and clearly, to empathize, and to authentically ask how I could be of service as others navigated the unexpected jolt as well.

3. The pause allowed me to reframe my thoughts about the upcoming year, to create spaciousness, and to engage thoughtfully. I could now ask myself new questions, and engage with curiosity.

I wonder what new pathways will open up for me that I would normally have to say no to because of previous client commitments. I wonder what new ways of working I can explore and experiment with over the coming months. What new networks, relationships, and spaces can I intentionally position myself in that I wouldn't have had the time for? What new questions will emerge that I didn't know to ask as a result of this surrendering?

This was a defining moment that required me to get comfortable with the following:

- disequilibrium: the unsteadiness that came from acknowledging that something was changing

- disruption as medicine: inviting in something new that was good and nourishing for me

- standing patterns: moments when I had to just wait

- holding and explicitly naming my purpose as a critical line of sight: an important requirement for embodiment in The ReSET Journey

Although I didn't understand its depth at the time, this moment positioned me in an elevated messy-middle journey. Here, the practice of holding a healthy tension between pausing and engaging became a normalized part of my daily practice. This new way to engage allowed me to lean in and surrender, rather than resist, leading the way to embodiment and one more milestone along the journey toward ultimately changing the game.

ReSET Condition 1: Get Comfortable in the Gray

These powerful words, "You have to get comfortable in the gray," from my executive coach, during my first-ever coaching session, left me speechless. In a single phrase, she named all my discomforts, pain points, and areas of "stuckness" as a leader. She invited me into an intentional relationship to stretch, grow, and release thinking, feelings, and actions getting in the way of my why and my purpose and preventing me from showing up to leadership self-aware, understanding the privilege of leading, and being poised to embrace transformational change.

I couldn't name it then, but today, I embody change and gray areas in my leadership—the places, moments, and situations that evoke uncertainty and ambiguity, and lack clear definition or easy answers.

Back then, I was in the messy middle of my leadership journey, the transformational space that revealed these three important truths:

1. The leadership walk can't be done alone. It has to be anchored in your unique purpose to resist the disorientation, distraction, and fatigue of this heavy work that you are leading.

2. Leadership is a walk that requires a level of intimacy with discomfort that can shift you through a range of emotions,

causing you to move from paralyzed and fearful to excited in the collective work.

3. This walk requires a coach who can ask powerful questions, support space for reflection, create accountability through action steps, and provide an open and curious space to grapple with fears, shadows, and unspoken ideas that have yet to be shared with the world.

My experience of the messy middle heightened my awareness of what's required of leaders working on the cutting edge of some of the most complex social issues of our lifetime. As you master your walk through the gray of the messy middle, you are armed with powerful questions that unearth new insights and interrupt false narratives. This space facilitates truth telling and offers permission to identify and name pain points for your ultimate healing.

The gray provides space to voice unspoken desires. It grants consent to align with your unique purpose. In the gray, your innate leadership is heightened, supporting a broader passion, will, desire, and clarity. As your comfort in the gray expands, your ability to exist in proximity to discomfort and your capacity to navigate the messy middle also expand. You grow exponentially in service to unleashing superpowers, catalyzing authentic partnerships, and resisting complicity. Consequently, your ability to mitigate harm to support transformational change within your key relationships increases. This enables you to innovate and lead in existing areas of your personal and professional life. Here, you can embody a stance that supports transformational change.

Given this proposition, I'm curious to know your answers to these questions:

1. In what ways do you believe getting in the gray could sharpen your ability to shift your thinking?

2. How can this space impact your feelings and actions to harness the necessary skills, relationships, and networks to generate the greatest return on investment as you tackle complex issues?

3. In what ways do you think your unique superpowers could be heightened in service to achieving key goals?

4. In what ways could getting comfortable in the gray enable you to change significantly in service to The ReSET Journey?

ReSET Condition 2: Lean Into the Power of Disequilibrium

Disequilibrium, a state of imbalance or lacking stability, is an essential part of the messy middle. The power of disequilibrium creates imbalance and dis-ease, a state where you feel off. It's that place where you're just about to fall, and consciously or subconsciously, you resist and then try to rebalance yourself.

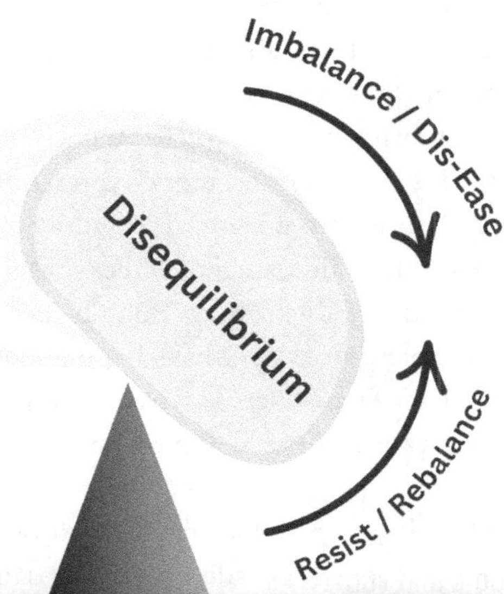

From the very moment I was introduced to the disequilibrium diagram, I was hooked. It gave explicit language to feelings and emotions I couldn't name but which were ever present in layers of the messy middle of transformation. The simplicity of this diagram provided powerful language for me to use to describe the roller coaster of emotions I'd been feeling. A strong commitment to a transformational journey fueled these emotions. I was challenged to develop a deep understanding of the hard places and the growing edges I needed to mine as I became aware of my resistance to knowing and understanding myself. I had unearthed feelings of complicity, sadness, and anger for holding myself back.

There were moments when I questioned my core values and beliefs and resisted my calling, times when I was ready to quit and create space for more comfort in my life. By not acknowledging these emotions, I ignored the intense toll this work had taken on me. By leaning into the disequilibrium, I was building new muscles, new ways of seeing myself, and new skills. I could forge new relationships that would carry me through the next elevated level of the messy middle of transformation.

The ReSET Journey requires you to practice and lean into embracing disequilibrium. It's a skillset that moves you from a high commitment to changing the game into a state of cognitive dissonance that raises new questions and introduces new realities. Disequilibrium invites you to make the invisible visible. This is done by continuously working to craft a more complete story of what's happening, what you're actually experiencing, what's factual versus what's merely a feeling.

Once you create a more complete story, you can't unsee what emerges from asking curious questions. Eventually, you begin to normalize this cadence in your daily walk. You become more open to the invitation being gifted by the situation. You can more clearly distinguish between facts and feelings

> Everything is information, and you have to treat it as such.

without judgment. And you can more easily create a complete story to inform your next best step.

What emerges is a new knowledge of the layers of your challenges, which stretches your ability to stay in the moment. Your ability to grapple with the dissonance is heightened. You notice where your energy and vibration operate from. You learn to resist being paralyzed from the discomfort and embrace action. You welcome the discomfort because you understand it presents valuable information to propel you forward. This discomfort creates the necessary conditions for you to bravely reveal and interrogate all the layers of who you are. Be ready because this emergence is clumsy; it's also necessary because it allows you to resist judging yourself and others. You merely take in the information as observations without judgment.

Everything is information, and you have to treat it as such. You have to suspend the urge to judge yourself and others and resist the instinct to make yourself a victim. This is where the process breaks you open at another level. Vulnerability makes an appearance. Suddenly, you're open to exploring new beginnings, possibilities, and truths. This further heightens your awareness and permits you to reimagine proximity, access, and boundaries. You arrive at a new place of freedom and liberation, where your commitment to change is a normalized practice. You incorporate this change into how you lead others. You apply it where new muscles, skills, and unlearning or relearning are modeled. This becomes a seamless part of who you are, which people experience when they engage with you.

The space between noticing a situation and trusting yourself to make strategic decisions gets smaller. Your capacity for social awareness is heightened, and your ability to regulate your emotions becomes a normal and powerful part of your walk. Now, you are continuously doing the work, and you understand—without question—that on the other side, you will be better for it. The work you do will be amplified, your collaborations will be more powerful, and the collective work will be elevated.

Imagine a gymnast walking across a balance beam covered with tattered tape and chalk marks left by a previous competitor. Suddenly, she turns to impress the judges, and she loses her balance. In an instant, a wave of energy rises in her, allowing her to self-correct. Her new balance—powerful and steady—shows up in the swing of both arms, the stretch of her legs, the arch of her back to move her forward, backward, and upward. That is The ReSET.

Now, she moves with greater awareness through the remainder of the routine. Deep, steady breathing gives way to focused concentration. In preparation for the dismount, she adopts a stance: mighty, undisturbed, confident. The previous misstep is but a memory, a learning, an input of information in the grand performance. With one step, then another, her momentum increases as she traverses the length of the beam. Her arms swing with grace and intensity, her final step solid, the power of her legs undeniable. Up, up, up into the air she climbs, twisting, turning, coiling—and then, she opens her torso, lands her feet solidly on the mat, and extends herself in full, chin up, eyes bright. She nails it!

Imbalance is necessary in the messy middle of transformation because it serves as a prerequisite for you to consider what's possible. You learn new ways of seeing and naming the emotions that come. The imbalance invites you to wrestle with the cognitive dissonance between what you know to be true and what's offered to you for new consideration. It gives you the necessary skills to persist through the discomfort and move toward embodiment of a game-changer posture. As you calculate the information provided by the imbalance, you can distinguish between what is challenging and what is hard. You intentionally create the space to practice, which enables you to successfully navigate and persist through the hardest moments.

This new posture sets you up to be present, aware, and clear and to anticipate the powerful incremental shifts that move you closer to a calling-forward state. These shifts help you get comfortable with the disequilibrium so you can view it as a powerful repositioning. After all, that disequilibrium must occur as a natural evolution within yourself and within your now and future story. Ultimately, this shift grants you permission to reconcile the cognitive dissonance that occurs from your old story so you can craft and embrace a new one.

Answer the following to assess how you're leaning into the power of disequilibrium:

- What part of your current story evokes feelings of disequilibrium? Where is there discomfort?
- What feelings are being revealed as a result of embracing disequilibrium?
- What new feelings or thinking do you need to embrace and/ or interrupt to lean into disequilibrium as an important part of The ReSET?
- What new freedoms are emerging as you embrace disequilibrium and discomfort?
- What or who do you need as a part of your circle to help anchor and ground you through this process?

ReSET Condition 3: Embrace Disruption as Medicine

Disequilibrium creates the space and possibility for disruption, and disruption intentionally makes the invisible visible.

Change was happening rapidly. One minute, I sat at a beautiful table with women from across the country, being pushed to dream bigger about my business strategy and invited into unfamiliar spaces I'd never considered through my role as a strategic thought partner on systems change, health, education, community economic development, philanthropy, and leadership development. The next minute, I found myself navigating and co-managing both the positive and negative backlash and stories emerging from a critical decision to pause this deep regional work with CoThinkk, which I, and a diverse group of women, had the privilege to be a part of.

For a decade, we engaged in deep collective work in response to anticipated changes in a national and regional backdrop that would undeniably impact our work moving forward. The rapid nature, turns and stops, and new information made it harder to anticipate what was next. Disruption is a healing balm and, as such, can sometimes be painful when first applied.

Now, I was being stretched in new ways. I was being broken open to the point where I didn't think I could expand any further. I felt weary. The evolution happened with such speed and intensity that I didn't think I could keep up. It was like drinking from a water hydrant and being asked to quickly make room for more.

As I described this complicated feeling to one of my close friends, she said I had missed what was waiting for me in the next big disruption. It was like I was holding my breath instead of normalizing the disruption as a part of a natural rhythm needed to propel me toward greater impact. In reality, the disruption consistently revealed new layers of my story and the places I resisted. I wanted to avoid those new places because they held the potential to raise my tolerance for change and for pivoting, adapting, and allowing for a deeper understanding of myself.

Disequilibrium heightens your ability to engage with your Now Story. It creates an amplified awareness for positive disruption to occur. Positive disruption is the critical medicine needed to move you closer to embracing embodiment of purposeful alignment and your purpose. It's the remedy that makes the invisible visible. When you see better, you can identify critical elements that facilitate bias, create discomfort and inequities, and limit innovation.

By creating the conditions to notice and name all parts of your story, you can actively interrupt, innovate, and redefine them. This new clarity allows you to tap into a power deep within yourself that has been cloaked in permission. You take the bold steps to activate your power, void of the need for permission. As a result, you transform your stories and align them with your life and purpose.

This intentional act of making the invisible visible acknowledges your power and agency. This critical step eliminates an antiquated way of thinking of power as holding authority over others. Instead, you accept true power is expressed by making explicit choices that anchor the values of collaboration, collective impact, seeding, nurturing, trust, and love. By anchoring the activation of power in these key values, you redefine the very idea of power and activate it as a means to share, wield, build, and transfer it in a new and evolved way. As such, others adopt the power to facilitate significant transformation, leading to sustainable change.

The activation of your power in this way, in the midst of disequilibrium, reveals the strategic path forward. Here, powerful emotions and readiness explicitly carve a clear line of sight to your purpose. By embracing disruption as medicine, you position yourself to courageously name your purpose in the midst of the messy middle of transformation. Now, you can move toward an elevated posture of embodiment and a more elevated, aligned, and truthful story.

Consider the following:

- What feelings are being revealed as a result of embracing disruption as medicine?

- What do you need to make visible and to name and notice in the midst of the disruption?

- In what ways do you need to activate your power—sharing, building, wielding, and transferring—to embrace the necessary enabling conditions in the midst of the messy middle?

- What strategic pathways are being revealed and moving you closer to naming your purpose?

ReSET Condition 4: Accept Holding Patterns as Necessary

Holding patterns are necessary to raise your vibration and emotional stamina to stay with and in the disruption.

I've been a passenger on many airplanes, and I always take note of those unique moments when the captain broadcasts that we'll be in a holding pattern in the air until we receive clearance to land. These moments of powerful pause are necessary to create the best conditions, put the right crew and partners in place, and align the timing to ensure a safe landing.

Holding patterns are a necessary part of The ReSET Journey. The holding pattern requires you to be patient and just wait for the clearing to come to ensure that the conditions for a safe landing are optimal. As you settle into this space, you build a deep trust that you're prepared to do what's necessary in service to the next leg of your journey toward embodiment. The holding pattern ensures you're on the best possible path to continue your evolution and safeguards you against negative actors, situations, and obstacles in your immediate path. Here, you are required to self-regulate so you're aware of your feelings that can inform your next best step while you stay the course on a designated path. Embracing the holding pattern, you learn to trust that if you miss your connection, an alternative course of action will be created and revealed.

In each holding pattern, you're required to stretch beyond your perceived limits. Stretching provides an opportunity for you to be still and reflect on your own journey toward purposeful alignment. It is in that stillness that you come to know what's required to raise your vibration and stretch beyond your perceived limits. When you're working at your highest and healthiest emotional state, you demonstrate positivity, optimism, love, and hope, as opposed to fear and resistance. This elevated vibration is experienced by others and offers a natural invitation for them to reciprocate.

I witnessed the effects of this principle as I worked through the power of permission with a dedicated cohort. During the online session, each attendee demonstrated an undeniable shift in body language. I saw the emotions building and the participants taking intentional pauses, going off screen to gather themselves, and coming back with heavy breathing.

Pausing, I shared some instructions: "Everyone, sit back in your chair."

Slowly and deliberately, each person complied.

"Now, take a deep breath, and as you do, give sound to your exhale."

A symphony of breathing filled the space.

I joined them, keeping my eyes on the screen for any indication that someone might be in emotional distress. Then, I asked, "What's being revealed at this moment for you?"

Silence.

This was a hard question, and I knew it, but thankfully, a few volunteers raised their hands.

Each brave volunteer, in turn, gave a response along these lines: "I wasn't prepared for the range of emotions I was feeling." That was their truth, and I understood it. They further explained that the invitation to yield to the emotion and to be aware of where that emotion resided in their body was a challenge. One participant stated it so clearly: "I wasn't prepared to name it and build the muscles to raise my emotional stamina and vibration so I could work at my highest level and navigate the journey of the messy middle."

These moments emerged with each cohort, becoming more intense and requiring an invitation to raise our collective vibration and build the emotional stamina to stay in and with the disruption. This type of holding pattern, where you have to wait for the lessons and essential information, sets the stage to enhance your ability to make critical choices. The space and critical moments gift you with the opportunity to pause, get quiet, reflect, and consider the labor you're using to prepare for the next big moment.

When faced with these holding patterns, I give myself permission to reflect, build new emotional muscles, and fail forward. This decision provides space to build greater awareness regarding my emotions. As a result, I can make strategic choices that enable me to raise my vibration for the next phase of the journey. The more I normalize this work, the more I'm able to amplify my vibration to the highest state in the Embodiment Journey. Thereby, I become a student working to master the enabling conditions that allow me to see clues and notice critical elements of my purpose and, therefore, prepare me to embody it.

As I sat at a crossroads on my journey, I felt off balance and uncertain, even fearful. At moments, I knew I was working at my lowest vibration as I moved through new and uncomfortable situations. I needed to stretch into a posture where my vibration was high and I felt certain, clear, and unapologetic. In these moments of stretching, I remained unwavering. I understood going back to the phase of my professional and personal life before I had chosen purposeful alignment was not an option. In that phase of the journey, I wasn't ready to consider my emotions and the ongoing labor required to manage the resistance that seemed ever present in the process of giving myself permission. Excitement, guilt, and forgiveness led me to lean further into transformation, even though becoming a game changer seemed far off in the distance.

Now that you understand the power of pausing, and that pausing is action, ask yourself these critical questions:

- What emotions are either holding you back or working well in service to raising your vibrations?

- What new awareness is being revealed to you as you pause, sit still, and reflect in a standing-pattern posture?

- What clues are being revealed to inform you of which conditions are necessary to help you move forward on this journey of embodiment?

Then answer these questions, which lay the foundation as you prepare to move fully into the idea of the stretch:

- What stretching is needed to reposition your stance to move from choosing to embodiment?
- What new questions are emerging?
- What questions do you need to grapple with?
- What new tools do you require?
- What new muscles have you built?
- What new growing edges and resistance do you have to notice and name?
- What unlearning and new learning do you need to embrace and continue to mine?

ReSET Condition 5: Explicitly and Courageously Name Your Purpose

The act of explicitly and courageously naming your purpose does not remove the discomfort, excitement, or fear of what could be possible and what is required of you as you name it, but it will create a clear line of sight for you moving forward.

Your ability to explicitly name your purpose in The Pause is critical. Remember, your purpose is your unique assignment or calling in spaces, relationships, initiatives, communities, and institutions, coupled with the intentional and strategic activation and positioning of your voice, unique role, and gifts.

The act of explicitly and courageously naming your purpose does not remove the discomfort, excitement, or fear of what could be possible and what will be required of you. Instead, naming your purpose enables you to resist the noise, distractions, and disorientation that naturally arise when you're moving through The ReSET Journey into an embodiment posture. Naming gives you the superpower—if you choose to accept it—to identify resistance in yourself and others.

When you name your purpose, you create a clear line of sight that raises your tolerance and improves your ability to recognize resistance while moving through it. By naming, you also attract those who support your journey. Allowing others to embed, integrate, and normalize conditions that cultivate success creates traction and elevation in your ReSET Journey. Naming your purpose in this powerful way begins the next step of the process and serves as an important guide, enabling you to embody your purpose and your game-changer posture.

Given this context, let's explicitly and courageously name your purpose using a three-step process.

Step 1. Establish your unique calling:

- What would you say is your unique calling, the thing you're compelled to do that no one else can do?

- How do you envision yourself when you strategically activate your voice around that unique calling? How are you moving when you walk in your calling?

- What are the unique gifts only you can extend to this world, your work, and the places, communities, and movements you engage with as a result of this vision and calling?

- What is your unique role in your calling? What is your position?

- What is your commitment? What are your driving values that create momentum?

Step 1: Establishing Your Unique Calling

What would you say is your unique calling, your "why," the thing that you are compelled to do that no one else can do?

How do you envision yourself when you strategically activate your voice around that unique calling? How are you moving when you are walking in your calling?

What are the unique gifts only you can extend to this world, your work, and the places, communities and movements you engage with as a result of this vision and calling?

What is your unique role in it? What is your position?

What is your commitment (your driving values that create momentum)?

Step 2. Put it all together:

{Purpose Exercise} - Formula + Coaching Questions

Use the previous prompts and the following formula for Purposeful Alignment.

 **Step 2: (UC + YV + UG + R + CE) * C = MC**

Your Unique Calling (UC)

> *Example: I feel called to encourage young people to believe in themselves.*

Intentional & Strategic Activation of Your Voice (YV)

> *Example: I do this by speaking up in my school, checking in on friends, and sharing positive words.*

Unique Gifts (UG)

> *Example: I'm good at listening without judgment and making people feel comfortable.*

Role (R)

> *Example: I see myself as a peer mentor and encourager.*

Compounded Experiences (CE)

> *Example: I've struggled with self-doubt, so I know how powerful it is when someone believes in you.*

Commitment (C) work

> *Example: I am committed to kindness, honesty, and consistency.*

My Purpose Statement (MC)

> *Example: By encouraging young people to believe in themselves (UC), speaking up and sharing positive words (YV), listening with compassion (UG), serving as a peer mentor (R), and drawing from my own struggles with self-doubt (CE), multiplied by my commitment to kindness, honesty, and consistency (C), I create momentous change (MC) by helping others feel valued and confident in who they are.*

Your Unique Calling (UC) + Intentional & Strategic Activation of Your Voice (YV) + Unique Gifts (UG) + Role (R) and + Compounded Experiences (CE) x Your Commitment (C) work = Momentous Change (MC).

Step 3. Explicitly and courageously state your purpose, and answer the following questions:

- What do you know about yourself now, regarding your purpose, that you didn't know before you began this journey toward embodiment of a game-changer posture?

  ____

  ____

- What feelings could get in the way of explicitly naming your purpose?

  ____

  ____

- What conditions (internal and external) do you need to mind and grapple with to continue to explicitly and courageously name and embody your purpose?

  ____

  ____

- What is one intention you're setting as you move into The ReSET Journey?

  ____

  ____

ELEVATED DISCIPLINE 2:

THE PIVOT: THE INTENTIONAL SHIFT

The second elevated discipline of The ReSET Journey is The Pivot. The Pivot requires a powerful pause to prepare for the intentional shift in your current story to move you closer to the embodiment of your purpose and a game-changer posture. Pivoting positions you to make an adjustment to gain a better vantage point. This new perspective enables you to interrogate each layer of your existing story to identify additional paths forward.

In the game of basketball, in order to pivot, a player must have a firm grasp on the ball. They then keep one foot planted on the floor while moving the other foot in any direction. Pivoting is a fundamental skill in basketball that allows players to change direction, protect the ball, and shoot or pass.

In The ReSET Journey, The Pivot is orchestrated as a strategic move. Most often, The Pivot is initiated in the face of a new awareness, new options and opinions, unexpected opponents or opportunities, or in preparation for a new vision. To set up an intentional transition in your story, consider any misalignment in your thoughts, feelings, and actions. These misaligned areas work against your ability to move from choosing to embodiment. The discipline of The Pivot sees everything as information, without judgment. A new set of questions are introduced at each layer of your story to provide clues and reveal new discoveries that enable you to course correct into the next leg of The ReSET Journey.

The Pivot is a natural component in this journey. It positions you to interrogate your existing story and the five essential story elements: characters, setting, plot, conflict, and resolution. Identifying these elements positions you to embrace a series of practices that normalize the exploration of the layers of who you are.

Ask yourself these questions as you explore these layers:

- What layers of yourself need to be acknowledged, embraced, and amplified to inform a new and elevated story?
- What components of your existing story allow you to move toward an elevated posture of embodiment?
- What layers of yourself need to be interrupted, redefined, and released to create a new and elevated story?

CHAPTER 5

S—SELF-AUTHENTICATE: THE NEW LAYERS OF YOUR STORY

This next layer requires patience, discipline, and willingness to peel back all the layers.

Self-authenticating is the third practice in The ReSET Journey. Self-authenticating is defined as confirming oneself to be real true, or genuine without requiring extrinsic proof or validation. This critical piece of the puzzle focuses on unapologetic curiosity and courageous truth-telling. By intentionally naming, noticing, exploring, knowing, and embracing all the layers of who you are, you identify your truest self at your core.

Do not try to rush this process. Self-authenticating requires patience. It takes discipline and a willingness to peel back all the layers of your current story. You need courage to sit in what's being revealed—resisting judgment—and decide to either lean in, resist, or embrace all the meaty nuggets. Consequently, you are gifted a unique opportunity to build muscles that enable you to understand and name the complex truths you learn about yourself. In addition, you build the muscles for awareness, tolerance, and emotional stamina to interrogate the layers of your existing narrative, both visible and invisible. These layers can position you to align with your story and to clearly articulate your purpose. Self-authenticating reveals powerful moments of truth-telling, fears, pain points, and opportunities, thereby setting the stage to take stock of your current and future story.

ReSET Layer 1: Unapologetic Curiosity: Revealing New Curiosities Through Each Level

What new curiosities are being revealed as you move through each level?

From the very first scene, the television show *Billions* captivated me. I hadn't heard of it until Damian and Jermaine Johnson referred to me as their Wendy. I was encouraged to watch it, and after the first episode, I was hooked. According to Investopedia, *Billions*, which premiered on Showtime in 2016, stars Paul Giamatti as a high-profile U.S. attorney with a streak of eighty-one consecutive convictions. Damien Lewis plays Bobby "Axe" Axelrod, a revered hedge fund manager and sole surviving partner of his firm after the terrorist attacks on September 11, 2001. The show explores themes of wealth, ambition, loyalty, and betrayal, blending sharp dialogue with complex character dynamics.[4]

The layers of all the characters are fascinating, but the character of Wendy Rhoades made me pause. A psychiatrist turned performance coach at Axe Capital, Wendy Rhoades (played by Maggie Siff) is often caught between her professional and personal loyalties. I find it interesting to watch her navigate the complexities of individual, company, and personal dynamics while showing up as a trusted source and motivator, powerfully holding space for everyone and every situation. At the same time, she grapples with her own self-awareness and vulnerabilities. She has so many layers. Just as I think I understand her, another layer reveals itself. My curiosity about her

---

[4] Julius Mansa (editor), "The Investopedia Guide to Watching 'Billions,'" Investopedia.com, May 9, 2024, https://www.investopedia.com/investing/investopedias-guide-watching-billions/

persona, coupled with a powerful question from Damian Johnson, led me on a quest.

"Tracey," Damian asked, "what parts of Wendy do you see in yourself?"

I sat with that question for quite a while. During my moments of reflection, my mind unraveled the many layers that revealed themselves as I yielded to the cyclical nature of the messy middle.

ReSET Layer 2: The Layers: Above, Below, and Deep

There is power in naming these layers and interrogating them as a critical part of this phase of the journey.

We've all seen that powerful image of the leadership iceberg, which differentiates what others see at the top from what's hidden beneath. Often invisible is the type of force, momentum, and motivation required to shift what's hidden to a more elevated state to meet critical moments of impact. In this journey toward embodiment, it's important to understand the messy middle creates a cyclical experience.

Above the Surface: What You Allow Others to See

When my colleague asked my opinion of the Wendy character in *Billions*, I paused to think deeply about my own layers. The people closest to me have commented that others who see my work most often see me as a very serious person: focused, intentional, and committed to building deep relationships. This is true. It's the authentic part of myself that I demonstrate above the surface. It provides a limited experience of who I am in the totality of Tracey from a holistic perspective.

The "above the surface" image is the first glance, similar to the first look at a wedding. The experience is relegated or connected to a moment in time, making it highly situational. It may represent the most comfortable place for others who experience you for the first time. It may support a narrative, fear, or unspoken expectation or insecurity they have created about you. As you explore the above-the-surface story and narrative, notice what curiosities are revealed about any alignment and misalignment regarding your current story.

Below the Surface: What You Know but Don't Acknowledge

My husband often shares that people are surprised when he tells them that, in addition to being quite serious in my work, I'm also a jokester who loves to play hide-and-seek. Most people are caught off guard when they learn I love to play. This sometimes disorients them as they spend more time with me. This truth raises multiple questions for me regarding which layers I'm willing to reveal and to whom.

I often go into deep interrogation when considering what is gained and lost by not revealing those layers, which lie just beneath the surface. I've asked myself what it would take to reveal those layers as I consciously and intentionally embody my purpose and stance as a game changer. Similarly, the Wendy character in *Billions* has the masterful ability to weigh the pros and cons in service to a larger goal. In every situation and relationship, she negotiates what is gained, what is lost, and where she has to pivot in the various roles she plays in pursuit of success.

In the same way, some of your traits exist just below the surface. These include the layers of you that you consciously know about yourself but don't want to acknowledge, as well as those things just out of your consciousness and revealed through triggers in specific situations. These below-the-surface traits whisper to you through what seem to be fleeting thoughts, opinions, and unconscious permissions you contend with on your journey through the messy middle.

Deep Waters: The Truth

Then, there are the deep waters—the emotional realm of the sub-conscious—where the unfiltered truth lies. Here, you find the candor regarding your true story and ultimately your true purpose, your why. This reality is hard to see clearly. It's the missing piece of the puzzle that allows you to craft a more complete story and explore every dimension of that story. Trying to embody your true purpose and alignment without immersing yourself into the deep waters of truth leads you farther from your true self, creating an unclear and incomplete story. In this deep place, you explicitly know and acknowledge your purpose. And when you know your purpose, you understand your Now Story includes what people see, what you know but don't acknowledge, and what's hidden, buried, or unconsciously taking up space.

Getting to the deep waters requires you to talk about your Now Story in the most honest and truthful way. By leaning into these deeper layers, you take stock of your existing story at the most intense depth, spotting the patterns, embracing what is revealed, and grappling with the totality of your Now Story. The outcome is to unearth the truth and ensure you align your truth with your real purpose. This process encourages you to speak your truth explicitly and courageously.

Answer the following questions to get a clearer picture of your layers:

- Which of the three levels (above the surface, below the surface, or deep waters) resonates most with you?
- What new curiosities does that layer reveal to you? What new questions do you have?
- Which layer is the place of your greatest pain point or growing edge?

- Which layer opens you up to what is possible and joyful?

- Where do you have the greatest momentum in resetting your story?

There is power in naming these layers. Interrogating them is a critical part of this phase of the journey. These layers are complex. They contain multiple mini stories that include a range of characters, settings, plots, conflicts, and resolutions. Once you consciously share, reveal, and interrogate those stories, you shift from a narrative for your eyes only to a narrative that invites others to experience it with you.

Answer these questions to dive deeper into ReSET Layer 2:

- What layers of your current story are you willing to interrogate deeply?

- As you interrogate the layers of your story, what patterns do you observe?

- What could allow you to lean in and work to know yourself at the deepest level? What could get in the way?

- What is your Now Story?

ReSET Layer 3: Taking Stock: Your Now Story

What is the Now Story circling in your head?

As mentioned, your story has five basic and equally important elements: characters, setting, plot, conflict, and resolution. These essential elements keep the story running smoothly and allow the action to develop in a logical way.

The characters in your narrative are the individuals your story is about. You can identify them with a detailed description of physical attributes and personality traits. In your narrative, you are the main character, and you determine how the plot develops, how problems are solved, and which supporting characters you enlist to move the story along.

The setting is the location of the action. It describes the environment or surroundings of your story in such detail that you can recall the scene clearly and vividly.

The plot, although tricky to distinguish within story and narrative, is easily identified by its ability to focus on cause-and-effect relationships. It doesn't just tell us what happened. It also tells us why an event occurred and what happened as a consequence.

Every story has conflict, which includes ways the character attempts to resolve the problem, and a climax, a turning point at the highest point of tension and emotion.

Lastly, the resolution is the solution to the problem, the way the conflict is resolved. It ties in with the overall narrative and creates an ending.

In resetting your narrative, you acknowledge that stories do not always run smoothly and are heavily influenced by messages, triggers, real life moments, other people, and the mental messages you send yourself. Ultimately, these messages reveal that you have the final choice. In order for this realization to occur, you have to integrate your Now Story, the story that you are currently in, and the posture from which you are making choices. Confronting your Now Story is the first step in resetting your narrative. It informs how you recreate your story, when and how to adjust your story, and how to arm yourself with the tools that allow you to ReSET your story to embody purposeful alignment.

The Now Story Exercise

NOW STORY

RESTATE YOUR PURPOSE

What narrative (the telling of a story) is being shared, experienced, or spoken
at this phase of your story?

CHARACTERS

SETTINGS

What narrative is being shared,
experienced, or spoken here?

What narrative is being shared,
experienced, or spoken here?

CONFLICT

PLOT

What narrative is being shared,
experienced, or spoken here?

What narrative is being shared,
experienced, or spoken here?

RESOLUTION

What narrative is being shared,
experienced, or spoken here?

Answer these questions to articulate your Now Story:

- Who are the characters at play in each layer?
- In what settings is your story playing out?
- What is the conflict, and is it internal or external or both?
- What is the plot of your story at each layer?
- What is the climax or tipping point? (This is that critical moment that changed or is changing everything for you.)
- What new questions, awareness, or information is revealing itself as the resolution in the face of the climax?
- What narrative (the telling of a story) is being shared, experienced, or spoken at each phase of your Now Story by you or others?

E—ESTABLISH: MAKE YOUR STORY COMPLETE AND CRAFT AN ELEVATED STORY

Create space to make a complete story by intentionally closing the gaps between the truth and the fiction in your story.

Establish is the fourth practice in The ReSET Journey and a courageous pivot that moves you intentionally from your Now Story to your more evolved and elevated story, one squarely aligned with your purpose. This pivot is focused on amplifying the lessons revealed during your self-authenticating process—both internally and externally—that clearly center your aligned and embodied purpose. It focuses on the establishment of a normalized new story. By naming the layers of your current story—interrogating what is true or false, what you see as a pattern, and what lies beneath each layer—you choose to make a more complete, more elevated story.

As you walked through the Game-Changer Principle in *Choosing Purposeful Alignment*, you leaned into the awareness of your story's true narrative, along with the choice to reset it as a vital part of your transformational process. This is critical to moving into a game-changer posture.

The story and the narrative you share with others may look different than the reality of your narrative. Your authentic narrative is for your eyes only, at least at first. However, you eventually must share it to move into purposeful alignment. Your narrative emerges from a series of related events and experiences, essentially, stories that can be true or fictitious. The true stories describe actual events you have experienced. The fictitious stories are invented or imaginary stories that help you visualize, dream, or clearly identify what you want or don't want for yourself in the future.

The Establish step is designed to create space for you to make a complete story by intentionally closing the gaps between truth and fiction in your story. You do this by revealing the often unspoken layers of your narrative. Giving voice to these layers enables you to make the invisible visible. This allows individuals, organizations, and communities to see your story from a more evolved lens. In essence, they see the aftereffect of you naming the often invisible elements that facilitate a biased story and elements that create discomfort and limit innovation.

Once you see these elements, you can interrupt, innovate, and redefine them in order to strategically play your unique role in the world. As a result, you activate your voice, talents, and wisdom in service to having greater impact. Now, you are positioned to play your ideal role in ecosystems of change by serving as a co-architect for the world you desire today and into the future.

As you make a more complete story, you'll find that you don't have just one big story; you actually have several mini stories that contribute to the larger narrative. These mini stories are often misaligned with your purpose, necessitating that you release them in order to effectively reset your story and align it with the new reality of your purpose. This begins with unmasking.

> What new story do I need to tell myself to activate this new and elevated story?
>
> What elements of my Now Story do I need to notice and name?
>
> What feelings will I need to interrogate in an elevated posture of embodiment and ReSET?
>
> This is what I know to be true.

ReSET Truth-Telling 1: The Unmasking

From the moment Brandy Mills started talking about her upcoming Woman Strong event in our hometown of Asheville, North Carolina, I was captivated by the theme that she chose: "Masquerade to Self-Discovery." The intentional action she called forward for everyone was to physically take off their mask. As I prepared to enter the space with these amazing women, I took note of the power in the language she used to center this experience. As I researched the origin story of the masquerade, and the mask itself, what I discovered was profound. I paused and grappled with what came up for me as I read.

The purpose of the mask is to conceal your identity, rendering you invisible. The mask, representing order and symmetry, is meant to allow you to break free from everyday norms and rules, releasing you to move in obscurity and allowing you to hide your identity so you can freely express your voice, emotions, and opinions.

As I readied myself to walk alongside this amazing group of women, I asked myself:

- What is lost when we render ourselves invisible to the world, in our relationships, work, and everyday lives?

- What is lost when we have to wear a mask that keeps us from moving toward freedom and liberation in our lives?

- What residue is left from hiding ourselves away?

- If we chose to truly reveal ourselves, would we recognize ourselves in the mirror? What would we see? What would be revealed that we refused to acknowledge?

- If the mask represents order and symmetry, where have we been complicit in hiding ourselves away? In what ways have we concealed the very magic of who we are, the unique layers that don't fit neatly in a box? (Hint: They aren't supposed to fit.)

- What happens and what is lost when we take on a persona, character, or identity that is not ours?

- What if expressing our feelings and opinions behind the mask creates or contributes to a false and antiquated story that keeps us from our purpose?

I invite you to explore the following questions in this moment:

- What is gained and lost by refusing to do the work and yielding to a posture of fear?

- What is gained and lost from being paralyzed and actively resisting your work?

- What counter resistance is required in the face of this resistance?

The unmasking is an invitation and another call to action. In this calling-forward posture, you move from the darkness into the light as the true and only reliable author and teller of your story.

ReSET Truth-Telling 2: Mini Stories and Archetypes

You don't have just one big story; you actually have several mini stories that contribute to the larger narrative.

I took a deep breath and logged on for my monthly coaching session with Dr. Towanna Burrous.

"Where have you been?" she asked in a direct voice. "Have you been avoiding me?"

I sat for a moment in silence, gathering myself, before I responded. "I wasn't ready. Our last coaching session broke me open in such a powerful way that I'm still processing it."

She patiently listened to me ramble about my lack of understanding about the stories people tell about me. I shared a specific story about women I had supported and the stories they now tell, months after I limited their proximity and access to me. As I expressed my confusion, I felt the disequilibrium take hold of me.

Dr. Burrous positioned her body on camera and leaned in intently before saying, "This is not new. I don't understand why you are so surprised that these patterns keep emerging. Pay close attention to the archetypes in this story, those patterns, behaviors, and traits that every human being possesses that motivate behaviors you consistently demonstrate. They're the same, but you keep missing it. Pay attention to the patterns and the characters that we and others adopt as we live our life stories."

I sat back and responded, "You're right."

In that moment, I knew that by being a truth teller, the distance between noticing, naming, and the truth would get smaller. The reality is that the mini stories would continue to show up over and over until I acknowledged the pattern, reconciled what was true and false, and embraced the layers of who I am. The mini stories generated through these patterns would eventually fade and become less relevant. They only served as information. I felt resolute that I was doing the work to interrogate and toggle between all three layers of my current story: what was visible, what was below, and the deep waters that housed the truth. As each story unraveled, another layer of myself was revealed. Learning valuable lessons led to naming the archetype present at each iteration.

The archetype is a persona that adopts behaviors that position us as the caregiver, creator, warrior, idealist, seeker, sage, realist, lover, or jester. Visible patterns, conscious and unconscious, emerge in truth. Each of the layers revealed clarity about who I was, in particular, the deepest layer. As I sat in this layer, I was able to reconcile the truth about myself and my story, to encounter multiple places and moments of realization and truth-telling. There, I began to grapple with and see where I was aligned and misaligned in my story when I juxtaposed it against my explicitly stated purpose.

Specific clues, patterns, and information must be revealed about the parts of yourself that you need to embrace as you create a new, evolved, and desired story.

As you seek alignment with the embodiment of a game-changer posture and embodiment of your purpose, I'm curious to know your answers to the following:

- What mini stories are playing out as you work to craft a more complete story?

- What archetypes keep emerging in each scene as you consciously reflect?

- What mini stories do you need to release to shift toward purposeful alignment?

- What lessons and nuggets will you need to embrace, dismantle, learn from, reconcile, repair, and celebrate to embody a more complete story?

- What will you need to embark on during this ReSET Journey toward an elevated posture of embodiment?

- What new story do you need to tell in this elevated posture of embodiment?

Pattern Spotting

What are you noticing?

Those four magic words of wisdom, "What are you noticing?" changed my practice and are the foundation of how I notice and name my experiences, myself, and the world around me. Those who know me well know I have a habit of keeping a list in my phone of patterns categorized by name, place, or situation. The notes section of my iPhone is my virtual diary, where I document in detail the dates, people involved, and reactions (mine and theirs). I use it as a tool to guide self-reflection, regulate my emotions, and grapple with what is true and not true. It allows me the spaciousness to wait for and notice (not react to) the patterns that repeat themselves in my engagements with others. It's all information, and it reveals lessons, behaviors, and greater awareness about myself and others.

It takes patience and pausing to spot patterns in the everyday moments, routines, and schedules to make the invisible visible. This regular practice arms you with the ability to make strategic decisions and choices based upon what you see documented and what you experience over and over again.

Unlearning to Relearn: The Reveal and the Lessons

The space between the noticing, naming, and documenting and then moving to action becomes shorter and shorter.

As the patterns reveal themselves, complex layers expose critical lessons, information, and truths necessary to propel you forward. The work to notice, name, and move to action requires you to embrace disequilibrium and the cognitive dissonance that comes with it. It requires you to embrace disruption as medicine as you name the patterns. You are driven to use choice and agency to glean the lessons that carry you forward to ReSET your story.

I had to build my muscle around it and reconcile what was true about my Now Story to move to my evolved story. The gap between noticing and naming what was true and what was fiction and my subsequent action got shorter as I interrogated each layer.

Each powerful reveal that emerged as I moved through this phase of the journey occurred in a pattern of four steps: noticing, naming, documenting, and moving to action. My good friend Bettie Hodges has told me over the course of my life that she noticed my lessons come quick and hard and repeat themselves. This was the case as I was invited to do that deep transformational work at all three layers.

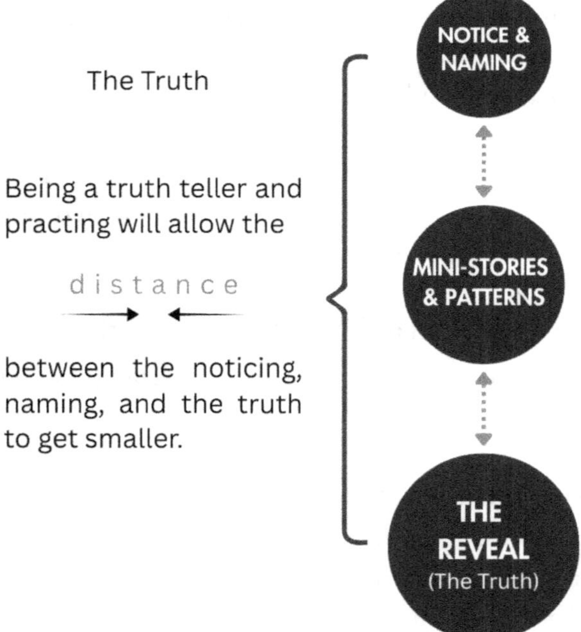

18 Months: Reluctant to See the Truth and Lead Accordingly

The first reveal took eighteen months. Everything inside of me told me this person wasn't a good fit for the work we were being called into. I understood at a deep level that we would need to transition this person, but because of how she was showing up, I was reluctant to do so. I believed I needed to put in place intentional support to ensure she didn't harm others in the same line of work and community spaces.

The team supplied support for her from two coaches who could relate to her culturally. Each coach provided a significant level of comfort and familiarity for the team. These coaches then walked the team through a repair process to ensure that if there was harm caused, we could create intentional space for healing, resolution, and transition. We also modeled clear expectations and articulated strategy, work plans, and the necessity to be present.

During a regular check-in two weeks earlier, I had communicated to this person that we would talk through each work plan and then move to implementation. On our next Zoom call, however, she said, "I didn't know I had to finish the work plan."

In that moment, a sense of calm came over me. The clarity that came with it allowed me to name the resistance and the truth that this person had no interest in doing the work. In that very instant, I knew that as long as I allowed this unhealthy dance to continue, she would continue to be the perfect dance partner. I didn't feel any anger, only relief and permission to shift.

This was the last pivot in the process, so I met with her in person, shared my appreciation for her contribution, and informed her we would need to end our partnership. My offer was a healthy and fair separation agreement. In addition, I made a strong recommendation with a national partner to provide a contract that allowed her to operate in the place she was most passionate about and talented in. Although I knew making this bold move was the appropriate action to take, I felt a little tired, but not exhausted. At this moment, the way forward was being cleared for essential work to occur.

Following that conversation, I sat with my team. They asked me hard questions about the process and why it took so long to end a collaboration that we knew at six months wasn't a good fit. The truth was that I'd been a barrier—and not in a good way. As they allowed me to unpack the hesitation I felt, the intense labor I extended in the process, and the reality of the impact, I had to sit fully in the truth.

My words filled the space: "Parts of her reminded me of me, a reluctant leader who wished she had someone to demonstrate how to pause, lean in, and provide support."

With that revelation came silence as they watched me process.

I added, "As a reluctant leader, when I received support in the form of mentorship, coaching, and opportunities to lead at the table, I was opened up in such a powerful way. It made room for the bloom."

As we sat in both the heaviness and lightness of this moment, I had to admit a part of me didn't trust myself. I questioned whether I had done all I could do to resolve the tension. I worried her transition would feed into a narrative already created about me by a small group of individuals who no longer had access or proximity to me, a narrative that I was unkind, unfair, and harmful.

As the meeting continued, my colleagues pushed through, asking a series of "But why?" questions.

I emerged with an awareness and knowing, which led to the following noticing and naming:

- This partnership wasn't aligned, and there was a gap in her skillset. We provided support that allowed her to be successful in a position where she could exercise her gifts and do work that brought her joy.

- I was patient, professional, giving, ethical, kind, and intentional in the support I provided.

- I provided extended support, wished her well, and indicated I would continue to support her work in the sector.

- I extended labor that potentially could seed something amazing and provide important muscle building for me.

- I ensured she was taken care of and I wished her the best.
- The negative outside narrative about me was held by the one percent. I needed to focus on the ninety-nine percent.

The new awareness also brought to my attention mini stories and patterns. I was part of the problem. An unhealed version of myself that wanted to rescue was playing a dominant role and preventing me from moving to action. That archetype didn't serve me well, but I hadn't been ready to address critical questions and new realizations.

There's power in The Pause and being in deep relationship with individuals you have the privilege to work with. My team had waited on me to receive these important lessons, although they had been ready to end the collaboration sooner than I was. They knew this was my work to do, and that doing so was critical to me elevating my stance as a leader.

I forgave myself and embraced the truth of who I am. I am clear about my purpose. I'm patient, professional, giving, ethical, kind, and intentional in my ask of how I can be of service. I'm trusted and have amazing truth-tellers around me, people who challenge and support me and wait for me to push through my growing edges. I'm flawed and always in a posture of reflection and learning, willing to take ownership of mistakes and assume a failing-forward posture. I am willing to be uncomfortable and to use my labor for a bigger cause and impact. I admit that sometimes the residue from that approach doesn't serve me well. Ultimately, I want everyone to win, to shine their light. It is each person's responsibility to move into the light when they are ready.

Six Months: A New Declaration

We had made sure the engagement was a good fit. As I sat with new colleagues in the back seat of the car en route to meet an amazing collaborative of community leaders, the first sign of misalignment revealed itself. The two colleagues were speaking to each other in a disrespectful way. It felt foreign to me as I sat there quietly observing the lead turn her energy toward me.

"We have concerns that you're not prepared, given that you couldn't meet with us on Sunday," she said from the driver's seat.

I paused for a moment to allow her words to wash over me. Then, I said, "I'm definitely prepared, and per our previously negotiated scope, we'd conducted our last planning meeting with your team and we were ready to go. I'd clearly communicated I was not available over the holiday weekend."

Rather than respond to me, she continued to drive, resuming a challenging verbal dance with her colleague in the front seat.

The second reveal regarding the true nature of this relationship and the leadership at the top came when the additional partners were left waiting. In their haste to remedy the situation, the leadership didn't ask for permission from the elders in the room to begin the meeting. This is a critical step in creating a respectful and safe space in grassroots engagement efforts. Following the meeting, she apologized as she dropped me off for my return flight.

"I know I didn't show up as my best self, and I will do better," she said.

For me, this was a signal to move forward and continue to focus on the work we had scoped out together.

The last reveal regarding the misalignment of this relationship and leadership structure came during a meeting. Zoom had always been an option, with specific exceptions. After six months of sending emails to try to schedule a call to ensure alignment with the plan, when this meeting came up, I was told in-person attendance was required.

As I moved into the space to take my seat, I greeted her, and I sensed the intense mental work occurring within her as she hugged me back. I greeted familiar faces, and then I positioned myself at the back table to be totally present and visible.

Leaning close to me, she whispered, "I'm surprised to see you here."

Without skipping a beat, and with a sly side-eye glance, I replied, "Well, I was excited to participate as part of our agreed-upon work.

You know that meeting my responsibilities is a top priority for me, and it's integral to being a good partner." I sensed her discomfort as she shifted in her seat.

She then leaned over and said, "We haven't had a chance to talk."

Without hesitation, I responded, "I would love for us to talk, and I have actively created multiple opportunities for us to share space to ensure clarity and alignment. When I reached out directly to our partners, they communicated that there was a different plan in place and I sent a follow-up email to you to gain clarity regarding how I could truly support the work moving forward."

I paused for her reaction, but she was speechless.

I continued, "I'm curious about the shifts and changes, as well as the barriers and what's needed to ensure we align our communication so I can truly be of service to your work. I need to know the best path forward so I can support you."

After a deep inhale and exhale, she leaned back in her chair and then forward again, as if ready for a confrontation. I waited patiently for her to build up the energy to express herself. When she did, she said, "Honestly, I didn't feel that you were prepared to move the work forward."

Surprised by her response, I paused and got curious, asking, "What parts of the scope, from your vantage point, am I not prepared to move forward with based upon our agreement? Please share with me. What is the barrier and where can I provide better clarity regarding the path forward?"

She visibly tried to formulate the best way to state what those areas were, but she couldn't. After a short pause, she said, "We're moving forward, and I want to shift your work with our partners."

And just like that, things shifted. As I took a sip of water, she hurriedly ushered over two leaders that I greatly respect, and we began to discuss how I could be of service. As we moved through the conversation, I was able to get to the next steps. I then indicated I would send a follow-up note after talking to the lead. As the table cleared, I shared that I would need to take a look at the original scope and assess the time and shifts necessary for me to commit to this new body of work.

In that moment, she pressed me. "Why can't you just say yes?

I shared that we had some unspoken issues we needed to address regarding how we worked together and what respectful engagement that honored each other's time looked like.

Then, she said, "Can't we just move past this and do the work together?" Those words dripped from her lips like honey from a spoon. They came at the very same moment as I heard the announcement that they were opening the Zoom rooms and they would be starting the presentation.

I slowly closed my laptop and packed my things to exit the space. I couldn't stay. Clearly, Zoom *was* an option when I'd been told it wasn't. I leaned over to her and said, "I'm about to transition from the space. It's clear we're out of alignment. However, I care deeply about your work."

With an undertone of anger, she said, "If you leave, Tracey, you'll regret it."

I leaned over and gave her a sincere hug, and then I exited the meeting before the full presentation began.

Her lack of communication, inattention to emails, and unwillingness to tell the truth about the availability of meeting options led me to believe she wasn't holding space for truth in this relationship. I contacted my assistant and had her arrange a seat for me on the next flight out.

I arrived back at the airport, which I'd just left an hour before. Before the wheels of the plane left the tarmac, I hit send on an email to her that spoke to the misalignment and stated our relationship hadn't been based in truth. As such, now was as good a time as any to end the partnership. I indicated I'd return the retainer in full, and I wished her well and mentioned I'd continue to support her work in the sector.

Later, as I prepared the certified envelope containing the check addressed to her office, the several truths emerged with clarity.

I noticed and named the following:

- I could trust myself. I had built critical muscles regarding noticing and naming behaviors that were misaligned with my values and practices.

- I had permission to interrupt those patterns while also continuing to address any growing edges being revealed for me.

- This relationship and this space were misaligned with my purpose.

- The story about my lack of preparation was false, and I refused to be complicit or normalize her behavior.

- I was never going to be a good fit for the project, and I was comfortable with that reality.

I observed these mini stories and patterns:

- I'd been intentional in ensuring the execution and the scope of the project.

- I'd given this situation enough space to breathe, and it was time to transition.

- The archetype playing out here was one of victimhood. My work was to name the misalignment and choose differently.

- Making a more complete story is part of my practice. Pausing, taking stock, and asking questions are all good. When these elements are balanced, I can allow enough time to process before moving to action.

I learned or relearned the following in the Reveal:

- Proximity and access to me are privileges. When those privileges were violated, I was poised to realign, set healthy boundaries, and pivot in a different direction.

- The work she was doing was important to the broader movement, and I would continue to support that work in a different posture, not as a strategic thought partner. Instead, I'd contribute as a silent supporter committed to deep work in the region, without judgment or negative comment.

- When you're committed to doing good work, and you demonstrate this in your walk, things always come full circle and your reputational and social capital is protected. Case in point, I was approached a year later with open sincerity and a request to reconsider partnering in the future.

Twenty-Four Hours: Can We Talk?

By the length of the text message, it was clear that there was a narrative being created about an emerging partnership. Unmistakably, that narrative was being designed to pit us against each other. We had been working, meeting, and breaking bread together over several months, building alignment, sharing values and operating principles, and dreaming together. So, this text came as a surprise. But because of the ways that we had been moving together, it created a level of curiosity versus a negative reaction.

I placed the call, and listened patiently to the situation before providing feedback to support her in making a more accurate story. I was able to quickly identify and name that she was operating from a place of fear. That fear had clouded her ability to see the complete situation.

"Let's get on Zoom in the next few days with all of the parties and work to make a more complete story," I suggested. My goal was to interrupt the false assumptions, feelings, and stories that were evolving.

From the moment we began the Zoom call, I could sense the nervousness from each of the partners. But I was at peace. I was clear and asked explicit questions, naming what I noticed and offering questions to help move us to resolution and to next steps regarding the partnership.

As I closed my laptop and took a deep breath, I knew several important truths (the Reveal):

- Being clear and naming the issues from a place of seeing a solution, a resolution, and what was possible was a part of my leadership style. This is how I show up unapologetically and my ongoing responsibility is to commit to continued growth and stretching in my imperfectness to embrace it.

- The work was too important to let fear, perceived competition, or the lack of a more complete story get in the way of a critical regional partnership that was needed as we moved forward.

- I refused to own the work that was necessary for them to do. They would have to do their own work and I would resist being complicit in a story of harm that had come from unresolved experiences with unhealthy partners. We were not the ones that had harmed them.

- I could fumble toward a repair process quickly, without judgment. Envisioning a deeper partnership was a win I wanted to celebrate.

- When I know what is true for me and what I want, no one is the villain, even when the situation—and others involved—are out of alignment.

- It's liberating to allow people to do their own work to have what they say they want. Freedom of judgment, not being a victim, and allowing others to choose their own path is true freedom.

- Be grateful you had a chance to be with them on that leg of the journey. Although the journey was hard, risky, and labor-intensive, it allowed me to make conscious, strategic decisions. I determined how much labor I would be willing to use in similar situations going forward. This journey built my muscles, not only for the moment, but also for the long haul as I continue to make intentional choices in the future.

As the gap closed from eighteen months to six months and then to twenty-four hours, the work and time needed to make a more complete story between each critical learning got shorter and shorter. As I moved into and embraced this elevated pivot that welcomed the intentional process of unlearning in an effort to relearn, the gap between truth and fiction also got shorter and shorter. Each experience revealed not only truth about the noticing and naming, the mini stories, and the lessons, but it also showed me the necessity to unlearn unhealthy habits, patterns, and behaviors that no longer served me. The result: I found that embracing a relearning posture provides important course-corrections along the way toward my embodied new story.

ReSET Truth-Telling 3: Moving from the Dance Floor to the Balcony

If you don't know David Dodson, then you should. He has a way with words and stories that create vivid images that birth beautiful frameworks that can hold complex concepts, language, and ideas. His constant aphorism is, "We have to move from the dance floor to the balcony."

In this process of repositioning, you are able to move from a place where you are most proximal to everything—the dance floor, right there in the middle of it all—to the balcony, which offers a different vantage point, perspective and viewpoint. In this process, you are repositioned differently.

There is power in normalizing the practice of The Pivot in this transition. The Pivot allows you to put into practice the process of unlearning to relearn. In The Pivot, you release the mini stories and move forward into the embodiment of being a game changer in your unique purpose. You move to a different vantage point and create space that acts as an invitation to deeply examine what was, what is, and what is yet to come. Now, you begin building a powerful groundswell of innovation, new practices, trust, healing, action, and new ways of seeing. This new position moves you into a posture of curiosity about yourself and others that resists any judgment about what you notice, name, and experience. You are ready to unlearn and relearn as the architect of your desired and future story.

The elevated pivot allows you to make the intentional choice that moves you from the dance floor to the balcony, and positions you just right to define, re-write and embody your new story. It may require a little dreaming to get there.

ReSET Truth-Telling 4: Re-writing Your New Story

The powerful pivot that leads to redefining and re-writing your new story serves as an essential defining moment in this journey and a bridge to dreaming. Dreaming is a critical bridge to defining your desired story and embodying it. Dreaming represents the start of manifesting what is possible and is meant to be the floor, not the ceiling. It is the precursor to a fundamental request for you to move to action in such a powerful way that activities align your dream in service to your purpose and your ability to re-write your story.

So, let's dream together and begin to re-write your new story by assembling the puzzle pieces to craft your new story, by first grappling with the following questions and dreaming exercise.

- What is the new, desired, and future story you want to tell and embody that is in alignment with your clear purpose?

- What healthy tensions exist as you release your Now Story and embrace your new story?

- What layers of your current story will you have to discard to make room for the new as you move through the messy middle?

Phase 1: Dreaming Exercise

The ReSET - Dreaming Exercise Diagram Phase 1: Part 1

Part 1: Restate your purpose as defined previously in our journey together through The ReSET.

Part 2: Dream about your new story.

- What is the unspoken dream that you carry in your heart and every part of your being regarding your purpose and being a game changer?
- How are you showing up in this dream? What is/are your role(s)?
- Who is there?
- What are/did you accomplish?

- What was/is different as a result of the role and position you intentionally play?

- What new narrative is being spoken about you and your work?

Part 3: Juxtapose your Now Story that you previously wrote with your dream for your new story. Put them side by side.

Part 4: As you dream and compare, consider the following:

- What are your non-negotiables regarding your layers and reveals as you envision taking the big seat, moving from the balcony to the dance floor?

- Dreaming represents the first phase of your process to re-write your story as you settle into The Pivot. The dreaming creates further permission to move you into the powerful re-writing of your new story and the subsequent narratives that will emerge as a result of the clarity, alignment, and boldness of the new story. The act of intentionally re-writing your story is a powerful step as you take your seat on the balcony.

Phase 2: Crafting Your New /Future Story Exercise

Part 1: State your purpose as defined previously in our journey together through The ReSET.

Part 2: Craft your new and embodied story. Remember, your story has five basic and equally important elements: characters, setting, plot, conflict, and resolution.

Let's take the next step forward through the new story exercise. Craft a new and desired story using the core elements of storytelling: the characters, settings, plot, conflict, and resolution. Answer the following:

- Who are the characters in your new/desired story? Include yourself as the main character.

- What is the setting or settings?
- What is the plot or purpose? (This is your purpose)
- What is the conflict (the issue that you are charged with solving/leading)?
- What is the resolution (the solutions, actions, and success that is resulting; name these explicitly) that centers your purpose as your clear line of sight?
- Name and notice the various roles or archetypes that are present in each of these layers.
- Name what you desire to be true in each layer and part of your story using the five elements of storytelling. Name what is possible through your embodied purpose.
- Name the resources, tools, and ways you will interrupt any patterns that may emerge that are not in alignment with, or in service to, your embodied purpose and game-changer posture.
- What is the final narrative—the telling of a story—being spoken at this stage of your new story about you and your work?

NEW STORY

RESTATE YOUR PURPOSE

What narrative (the telling of a story) is being shared, experienced, or spoken
at this phase of your story?

CHARACTERS

SETTINGS

What narrative is being shared,
experienced, or spoken here?

What narrative is being shared,
experienced, or spoken here?

CONFLICT

PLOT

What narrative is being shared,
experienced, or spoken here?

What narrative is being shared,
experienced, or spoken here?

RESOLUTION

What narrative is being shared,
experienced, or spoken here?

ELEVATED DISCIPLINE 3:

EMBODIMENT: THE FORWARD STANCE

The third elevated discipline of The ReSET Journey is Forward Stance. Forward Stance requires you to move from an elevated position as an embodied game changer. From this position, you actively and consistently align with your clear purpose and you own the authorship of your new story. Now, you lean in from your core strength. This requires energy, will, drive, focus, and strategic activation so you can move toward embodiment of your new, desired, and future story.

In *Choosing Purposeful Alignment: The Messy Middle of Transformation*, I introduced the core elements necessary to move to an embodied transformation state that's lasting and offers a continuous space to activate what's possible when you embody your purpose. This process invites you to normalize, embed, and practice the following four critical elements in every part of your being: stance, energy, rhythm, and awareness.

Stance is your physical orientation to the world. More specifically, it positions you to be clear about what you want to do and what is standing in your way. During transformational changes and embodiment, your stance must be forward facing and directionally balanced. Forward Stance demands a different way of being. In this position, you are not focused on emphasizing protection, pushing back, or preventing things from happening. Instead, Forward Stance promotes shifting intentionally to the offensive and moving to a position of core strength.

In the game of basketball, after the pivot, it's imperative to assume a forward stance to make the final shot that brings success. This movement requires you to be clear about stance as you hold the ball firmly in the face of moving opponents and a game clock that's winding down. You must make strategic decisions regarding the best path to the goal, whether to use your strength to shoot a three-pointer, or whether to power your way through countless bodies and make an intentional layup or dunk. Whichever choice you make requires three elements: energy, rhythm, and awareness.

These elements were first introduced to me by Erin Byrd, in 2017, through a collaboration with CoThinkk as she moved us through a process to examine what was necessary to facilitate lasting change and impact in movements tackling complex issues. Through this invitation, my lens regarding transformation forever changed. In a similar approach, Zen teacher and thought leader Norma Wong's principles on strategic thinking focus on understanding, strategically moving, and activating energy to propel or attract people, situations, partners, ideas, innovation, and opportunities.

In its most powerful form, energy aligns and embodies purposeful alignment. Energy can spur people to support a cause, rise above challenges, and become active participants rather than passive bystanders. The concept that "like attracts like" is true for both positive and negative energy. When your energy is negative, you are drawn to situations, relationships, and issues that reflect where you are in the moment. Conversely, when your energy is positive, you align with opportunities that match your thriving and dynamic energy. That brings us to rhythm.

The elevated discipline of Forward Stance recognizes the rhythm within and around you necessary to ensure a sustainable pace on the Embodiment Journey. According to Byrd and Wong, a suitable rhythm recognizes the different paces, builds in phases, and intentionally manages restorative pauses. When rhythm is too fast, too slow, erratic, or doesn't pause, your stance shifts and you become out of balance. When you're in sync with your rhythm, you create a deep awareness that enables you to pause. This allows you to yield to the temptation to push on beyond your limits, while creating the optimal environment to sustain momentum.

In basketball, being aware of your rhythm, and gaining mastery of it, is critical in nearly every function of the game, from bouncing and handling the ball to positioning your hands for the best possible shot, regulating your breathing as you watch the movement of teammates and opponents on the court, or gauging the right moment to move toward your envisioned outcome. All of this requires awareness, another important part of the equation in this formula.

During our collaboration through CoThinkk, Byrd emphasized that Forward Stance requires a keen sense of awareness, the perception of what's happening around you. Your awareness is ideally as broad and objective as possible, inviting you to consider all possibilities and forcing you to see, think, and process your understanding before you act. With a keen sensibility, you gain more awareness by being connected to your body, understanding yourself, and understanding the perceptions of others.

This element is the most important. Without an acute awareness, it's hard to adjust your stance, balance your energy, or even be aware of your rhythm to unapologetically activate your new and future story. If you are not actively connected to your body, you cannot know your natural rhythm and how to adjust it. How can you activate this new way of being as a game changer and truly embody your purpose and game-changer posture?

Your mastery of this elevated discipline helps you evolve, sustain, and amplify the shift from choosing to embodiment as you close the gap between your Now Story and narrative and your new story and narrative. Here, you have the constant fuel and momentum to inform, align, and catalyze your ongoing and future story that aligns with embodied purpose and game-changer posture. This is bigger, bolder legacy work, anchored in deep intentionality.

CHAPTER 7

T—TALK ABOUT IT: ADJUST AND REPOSITION YOUR STANCE

What new story will you tell in this elevated posture of Forward Stance that moves you closer to embodiment and ReSET? What will you need to fully stand in it?

There is incredible power in being a storyteller and talking about your story out loud. Talk About It is the last step in The ReSET Journey. It represents the unapologetic owning, embodying, and celebration of your embodied story of being a game changer and purposeful alignment. It serves as a visible and public reintroduction of yourself to yourself and to the world. Here, the space as a storyteller focuses on leveling up and embodiment. Rooted firmly in this stance, you're constantly invited to shift, pivot, heighten your awareness, and adjust your energy and rhythm in service to a Calling-Forward posture and Forward Stance.

ReSET Stance 1: Own Your Story

From the very moment I talked to her over the phone, I saw something special in who she was and what she was destined to do. Her cousin had referred her to my Aligned Intensive Course and I quickly connected with her as she prepared to move into the course with other cohort members from across the region. As an entrepreneur, she was clear that she was ready to level up her business and join me for additional coaching sessions outside of the course experience.

The first time she joined me on Zoom, her facial features were undetectable. A dim light from a small lamp on her desk and the window behind her created a silhouette around her frame.

"I can't see you," I said, hoping she would shift her position.

She responded, "I'm present, working hard, and listening."

As a coach, I constantly adjust the ways I walk alongside and ask powerful questions in service to moving client partners forward. As I observe them, I intuitively know when to give them space to breathe. In this moment, I knew I needed to activate and tap into all three movements—energy, rhythm, and awareness—to experience what could be possible if I met her exactly where she was and gently ushered her forward.

She slowly moved into the light . . .

She grappled with her fears and her hesitations because she was challenging herself and moving into unknown territory, her messy middle.

She asked herself out loud, "What new thinking, feelings, and actions do I need to pivot and evolve as an entrepreneur in order to level up?'

This was powerful because, as we know, our thinking impacts how we feel and our feelings impact our actions.

And with each session . . .

She revealed more and more of herself. By our third session, although she was still mostly in the dark, I could see her facial features. By our fifth session, she was fully visible, but her room was still dark. By our last three sessions, she stepped into the light—the light in the room and the light inside of her.

Her answers to her own question helped her know her purpose, her strengths, and her significance.

She allowed herself to be seen, to be heard, and to know who she was in all her layers. Her intentional and incremental journey enabled her to grapple with her layers, practice and normalize disequilibrium, and disrupt the mini stories that didn't serve her. Her ability to see pausing as action and to embrace a holding pattern of noticing and naming, allowed her to elevate in ways she didn't realize were possible.

She has since started and grown a successful consulting firm focused on partnering with corporations to build new muscles, tools, and practices that center equity, diversity, and inclusion. In this Forward Stance, she became more visible, amplified her voice, practiced stretching beyond her perceived limits, built capacity to engage in hard conversations, normalized being uncomfortable, and integrated unwavering courage, transparency, and vulnerability in her everyday walk.

She also began to own her story and share it with others. This process redefined what was possible when she intentionally removed her mask, crafted and told a new story for herself, and ultimately released her baggage in order to embody her story. The process of owning her story by talking about it openly and unapologetically was the repositioning she needed to ultimately change the game through a more aligned and embodied story that amplified her purpose.

ReSET Stance 2: Embody Your Story and Change the Game

On the other side of hard is magic.

The hard part is the intentional work required to move through the messy middle of transformation to ReSET your new, evolved, and aligned story. The magic is the demonstration and visual impact of how you're changing the game in this new posture as a game changer.

The game is any story, complex issue, system, lever, circumstance, relationship, or space that must be innovated, interrupted, evolved, dismantled, or configured in service to deep impact and transformational change. The new story, one aligned with your purpose, allows you to pivot, assume a Forward Stance, and stand in it to reveal the magic.

"I can't meet you there and I won't meet you there." This was my response to a relative attempting to pull me back into an old pattern with them. I had previously communicated this way of interacting wasn't healthy for me and I wouldn't consent to the chaotic and often dramatic dance used to create conflict and a manipulated outcome that centered their needs.

As the words left my lips, I continued to stand fully in the freedom of the evolved story and embodied posture of a game changer. The cadence and intentional telling of my new story were amplified through an embodied stance focused on a clear line of sight. I was committed to moving forward and working to change the game.

This type of clearing allows for true liberation from stories, relationships, or places out of alignment with your clearly stated purpose. As you continue to elevate at each stage of your life, leadership, work, and relationships, this clearing occurs. As you own and tell your new story, and stand in it, the path forward is etched deeply into every place, relationship, and body of work you choose to engage with. This clearing reveals the evolved archetypes that become a seamless part of how you move into every space.

As a result, you exude the following from your very being:

- You own who you are at your core and accept permission to evolve.

- You embrace the truth that you have agency and autonomy to choose self and work.

- You come to terms with who you are and resist the need for validation from others.

- You demonstrate courage and bravery.

- You model what it means to show up as your best self and you desire the same for others.

- You walk in honesty and transparency.

- You normalize fumbling toward creative reparative cultures, where you wrestle with the issues.

- You accept that this work is constant and cyclical. You have to choose it every day.

- You adopt a stance that practices collective power and shares, builds, wields, and transfers power back and forth.

- You resist complicity and choose to move in solidarity with and work alongside leaders and communities who you support as a privilege.

- You wrestle with the issue and not with each other, resisting the seductive snare that keeps people separated from one another and trapped in false stories.

- You cultivate a circle of friends and colleagues who are a part of the medicine that feeds you, and you feed them in return.

- You limit proximity and access, without judgment, for individuals, places, or spaces that are out of alignment.

- You understand you don't have to use your energy to convince because your language becomes an invitation for others to choose.

- You give yourself permission and lean into ongoing transformation and evolution.

- You normalize an ongoing practice of reconciling what's true and what's not true to create a more complete story.

- You set clear boundaries, not as a means to keep people out, but to invite the right people and experiences in, holding space for them.

- You see your fear as power and embrace the opportunity to engage with it deeply as a means to stretch and grow.

- You notice when the time, place, and approach are in alignment as foundational components in every relationship.

- You're mindful of your labor and how you transform and activate it.

The freedom to walk in your new and embodied story is a reward that necessitates honoring this significant moment of intentionality, energy, and labor.

ReSET Stance 3: Realign Your Labor + Energy + Restorative Pauses

Stepping into and fully integrating this embodied practice requires the ongoing assessment and inventory of both the visible and invisible use of your labor and energy.

This powerful Forward Stance doesn't come without effort. To practice, stretch into, and sustain this stance and elevated discipline requires labor, energy, and restorative pauses.

I kept saying for weeks to my husband that I was tired and couldn't figure out why. I inventoried all the ways I took care of myself. I walked every day, I took my daily vitamin and energy regimen, and I was mindful of my calendar. But as I ventured on my walk one Sunday morning and reflected on a recent Purposeful Alignment Women's Experience, where we grappled with issues of labor and energy, I had an epiphany.

I realized holding this elevated Forward Stance required a new level of labor, energy, and restorative pauses. It required a new awareness moving forward, one that invited a new layer of consciousness and restorative practices. Here, I had to name the visible and invisible labor and energy required to move forward and lean into the necessary respite.

Labor. Stepping into and fully integrating this embodied practice of purposeful alignment requires the ongoing assessment and inventory of both the visible and invisible use of your labor and energy, compelling you to ask how, when, where, and with whom you use your labor and energy. Labor is the physical or mental effort used—consciously or unconsciously—especially when something is hard or required. It's natural to notice and name the visible labor, such as your career, attending meetings, and scheduling. Yet, an entire layer of invisible labor often goes overlooked, like the emotional support, strategic planning, and continual mental tracking that quietly sustain individuals, teams, families, communities, and organizations.

In the 2021 BBC.com article "The hidden load: How 'thinking of everything' holds mums back," by Melissa Hogenboom, researcher Allison Daminger names four key stages that capture the nuance of this hidden workload: anticipating needs, exploring options, deciding, and monitoring.[5] As you inventory where you use your labor, notice that "hidden" and "invisible" labor are used interchangeably. We define hidden and invisible labor as the type of labor kept out of sight or concealed. Daminger describes it as the invisible work performed internally, making it difficult to know where it starts and ends. You are less conscious of how you use it. Like the air you breathe, you don't see it, but you still feel it.

Invisible labor is concealed, even from yourself, and can be cloaked in unspoken expectations held by you, society, community, and others. It's not until you pause, look inward, or reflect with 20/20 hindsight that you see it. By recognizing the visible, invisible, and hidden aspects of your daily responsibilities, or labor, you open pathways for recalibrating priorities, reclaiming energy, and moving toward more aligned and transformative outcomes in the embodiment of your purpose.

Energy. While labor focuses on the mental and physical effort required to complete a task, I define energy as the physical, mental,

---

[5] Melissa Hogenboom, "The Hidden Workload: How 'thinking of everything' holds mums back," BBC.com, May 18, 2021, https://www.bbc.com/worklife/article/20210518-the-hidden-load-how-thinking-of-everything-holds-mums-back

and emotional resources and internal capacity to handle those tasks and demands. Energy and labor go hand in hand, and you must consider and examine each one daily as an intentional part of the practice to evolve, sustain, and amplify the embodiment of your new story.

Having agency over how you manage your energy is critical. According to behavioral scientist and author Jason Hreha, the key to lasting change is to "optimize your energy" by addressing your personal "energy bottlenecks." This is a key theme in his book, *Real Change: Moving Beyond Habits to Achieve Lasting Transformation.*[6] Hreha defines an energy bottleneck as anything that makes you feel drained, exhausted, or unable to make progress. These obstacles prevent people from starting new practices or routines. While the specific drains are individual, Hreha emphasizes identifying and addressing them rather than relying on sheer willpower, an overrated and unreliable resource.

Based on his numerous podcast interviews and discussions in 2023, drains include:

- Trying to force an unsuitable habit: Attempting to implement a habit that doesn't fit your personality, lifestyle, or goals, such as forcing yourself to run an hour a day when you hate running.

- Relying on habit hacks: Believing minor tweaks and reminders are enough to drive significant behavior change, which Hreha argues is a fundamental misunderstanding of how change actually happens.

- Failing to address foundational energy issues: Ignoring issues like poor sleep, which depletes your overall capacity for transformation.

- External distractions: Constant consumption of media and being pulled in too many directions, instead of being a focused creator.

---

[6] Jason Hreha, *Real Change: Moving Beyond Habits to Achieve Lasting Transformation*, (Jason Hreha, 2024).

- Ignoring qualitative feedback: Focusing solely on metrics and numbers without listening to qualitative feedback from people involved, which can be a key source of insight.

Instead of relying on simple hacks, Hreha advocates creating practices that better fit your individual needs and personality. These more mindful actions recharge your energy rather than drain it.

Potential recharge sources or practices based on Hreha's work include:

- Mindful engagement: Engaging in activities that feel meaningful and are deliberately selected to align with your personal needs and goals.

- Strategic behavior selection: Choosing the right behavior for you, instead of adopting the popular or what works for others (lifting weights instead of running, for example).

- Taking a flexible approach: As a non-routine-oriented person himself, Hreha highlights the importance of flexible schedules and practices, such as working out when you feel like it, rather than at a fixed time each day.

- Creating, not just consuming: Hreha has previously written about reclaiming humanity by becoming a creator rather than a passive consumer.

By knowing what activities, people, and spaces drain or recharge your energy, you can strategically balance tasks, prioritize self-care, and advocate for changes to create a more sustainable and fulfilling professional and personal life. This proactive approach fosters greater productivity, reduces stress, and enhances overall health and happiness. Balancing, integration, and management of your energy alongside your labor are critical as you operate in an elevated discipline. This is how you support the story and narrative aligned with your embodied purpose and game-changer posture. Let's inventory your labor and energy.

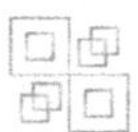 *Re-imagine Labor* | Instructions

List Tasks: In each category box, list everything you do—large responsibilities and small, everyday actions. Use scratch paper if you need more room.

Mark Time & Stress: Next to each task, use the Key to note how much time it takes and how stressful it is.

Check Necessity: Now that you see the total cost, decide if each task is truly necessary. Can you skip or simplify it?

Determine Ownership: Who should own this task—you, someone else, or can it be delegated? Was it pushed onto you unfairly?

Reclaim Your Energy: Look at what you've freed up. How will you use that extra time and energy to center yourself?

DEFINITIONS

<table>
<tr>
<td>

Emotional Labor:
Managing your own and others' feelings (empathy, support, conflict resolution).

</td>
<td>

Domestic Labor:
Taking care of people and tasks (cleaning, cooking, childcare, eldercare, errands, yard work, etc.).

</td>
</tr>
<tr>
<td>

Coordinating:
Scheduling, planning (appointments, events, meals, etc.).

</td>
<td>

Mental Load:
Constant mental tracking and preparing, organizing and anticipating everything, emotional and practical, that needs to get done to make life flow.

</td>
</tr>
</table>

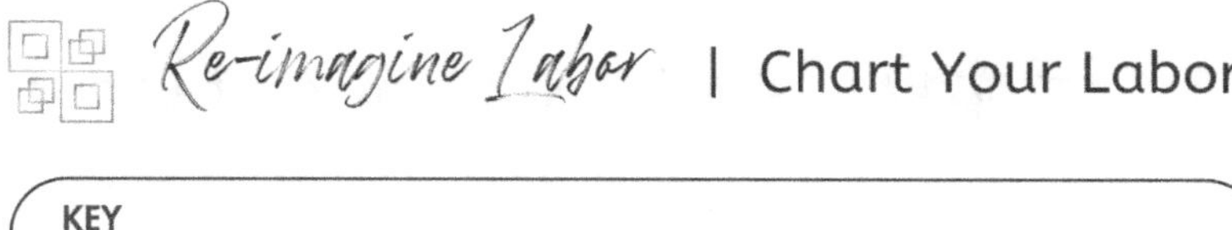

Re-imagine Labor | Chart Your Labor

KEY

Time? Enter days, hours, minutes.

Is this necessary? MD - Must Do, **SK** - Could Skip, **SI** - Could Simplify

Stress/Energy? L - Light, **M** - Moderate, **H** - Heavy

Ownership? M - Mine, **S** - Shared, **D** - Delegate, **N** - Not Really Mine

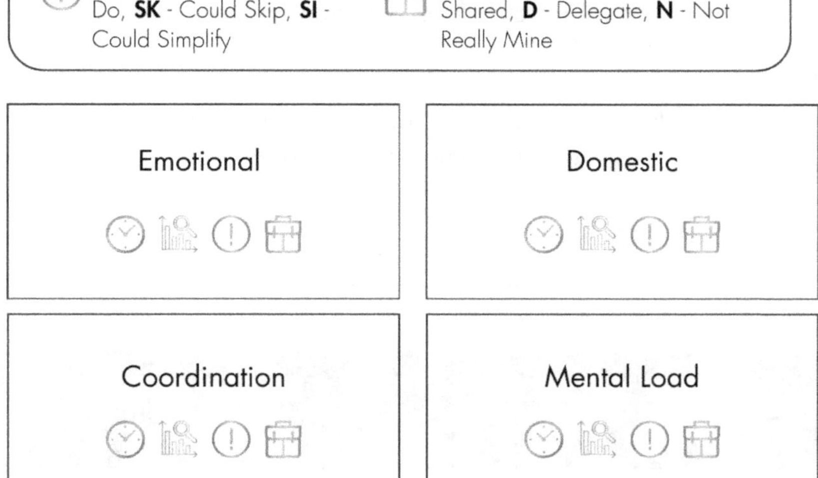

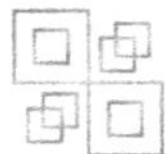 # *Re-imagine Labor* | Reclaim Your Energy

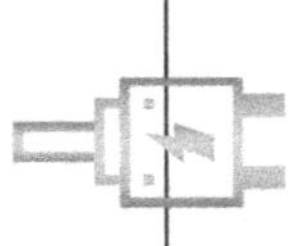

How much of your labor is hidden and invisible?

If you re-imagined your labor, which labor would you use towards your own transformational journey?

In what ways would you direct that energy towards fulfilling your own purpose?

I'm curious to know:

- How much hidden and invisible labor and energy do you use in your current posture?

- If you reimagined where you use your labor and energy, which labor would you use toward the embodiment of your new story and your new posture of an embodied game changer?

- In what ways would you direct that energy toward fulfilling your own embodied purpose and new story?

- As you lean into embodiment and inventory where you actively use your labor, what would be possible if you shifted the labor you use every day to center yourself and move further along your Embodiment Journey?

- When you actively and intentionally move in this way, how does it support and amplify your elevated discipline and the Embodiment Journey?

- What powerful choices regarding energy and labor will sustain this new elevated posture and discipline?

- When will you take aligned action to propel you further, faster, and deeper into your new embodied story and narrative?

Restorative Pauses. The conscious choice to reallocate your labor and energy to grow into and sustain this elevated discipline requires restorative pauses. Restorative pauses are short periods of relief that provide respite when you're stretching into and working at this new elevated discipline. The restorative pauses invite you into an ease and intentional resting period—a brief one—that allows for different types of rest.

From the moment I saw her TEDx speech, I was obsessed with Dr. Saundra Dalton-Smith's transformative invitation to rest. She shared seven types of rest: physical (active or passive), mental, emotional, social, sensory, creative, and spiritual.[7] The language she provided serves as an important and ongoing emergent discussion and practice in this elevated discipline.

It requires exploring some powerful questions: (1) Where, when, and how do I intentionally tend to the physical, mental, emotional, social, and spiritual aspects of myself? (2) How can I use rest in a transformative process that results in positive impact, self-realization, and embodiment?

These questions invite additional reflections, strategic choice points, and decision-making about where you extend your labor, energy, and will, while creating space for restoration.

I'm curious to know:

---

[7] Shaundra Dalton-Smith, "The real reason why we are tired and what to do about it," TEDx-Atlanta, April 9, 2019, https://www.youtube.com/watch?v=ZGNN4EPJzGk

- When will you actively and intentionally take these three dimensions (labor, energy, and restorative pausing into account while on this journey? What will that look like?

- What permissions and powerful thinking do you have to embrace to consider labor, energy, and restoration alongside your embodiment posture?

- As you lean into transformation, from whom in your circle of influence do you need permission, support, or affirmation?

- What powerful actions will you take to lean into this yes for yourself?

- What fears do you need to name and overcome to stay the course?

ReSET Stance 4: Let Go of the Baggage

Crafting your new story in this Forward Stance serves as liberation to release the past and move toward the future. Consequently, the experience evokes emotions, valuable lessons, and powerful questions as a natural outcome of this intentional process. What fears and baggage could get in the way of the embodiment of this new and accurate story? For me, the baggage and fears came in the form of Ayden and the work it took to name those emotions and release them in service to my new embodied posture and purpose.

It took me more than ten years to share the gift of Ayden with the world. This story has been like a pregnant pause, one in which you know you're carrying something so special within yourself, but you've yet to announce it publicly.

Ayden was my firstborn son, born on Valentine's Day, 2009. Ayden's powerful birth and death taught me many lessons about fear, releasing baggage that no longer serves me, and what it takes to work at an elevated discipline and embodied posture. One of the first lessons he gifted me is that interruption and disruption are part of a necessary first step. Throughout the walk on The ReSET Journey, this becomes a foundational component, inviting an awareness and shining a light on the hidden stories, voices, and clutter taking up space.

The second lesson I received was the understanding that clearing space is necessary to prepare for change. This powerful purging process opens the way for new stories and releases you from the mask so you can see the now with fresh eyes.

The third lesson was acknowledging that feelings and grieving are necessary. They invite you to surrender to and accept patience and forgiveness. Lastly, the most powerful lesson Ayden gifted to me was redefining what is hard.

Ayden's conception and birth created a catastrophic event that forever changed me and the lens through which I saw myself in this world. His conception, birth, and transition continue to inform how I perceive and define hard. I used to think everything was and had to be challenging and urgent, between an eight and a ten on a ten-point scale. "Ayden hard" is a ten. Everything else is a challenge and lives around the three-point mark. This perspective has allowed me the gift of resisting being paralyzed by difficulties. Now, I embrace the gift of noticing and understanding patterns without judgment, I make decisions and pause when necessary, and I continue to do my work to know the difference. Ayden's gift is present when I'm faced with any challenge. The critical cue I now use is a simple question: "Is this Ayden hard?"

Everyone has different baggage, fears, and powerful moments that create new paths or course corrections. These moments are parts of your Now Story that propel you into your new, evolved story. With them, you form powerful memories and learn lessons that either move you forward or hold you back. Your work is to view those moments as gifts to support your forward motion. When you resist the disempowering beliefs that emerge at every corner, you position yourself for radical celebration. In this way, you embody what it means to be a game changer and to live in purposeful alignment. In order to be in radical celebration, you have to address your fears and disempowering thinking and then make conscious decisions about the labor that could get in the way.

Interrogating Your Baggage Exercise

Answer the following to assess the baggage that may be standing in your way:

- What fears may be getting in the way of embodying your desired or future story?

- What fears and baggage are standing in the way at this moment?

- What powerful thinking has emerged regarding your fears and baggage? What is true and what is false about each thought?

- What powerful feelings are emerging as a result of acknowledging these fears and baggage? What is true and what is false about each feeling?

NAMING & INTERROGATING FEAR

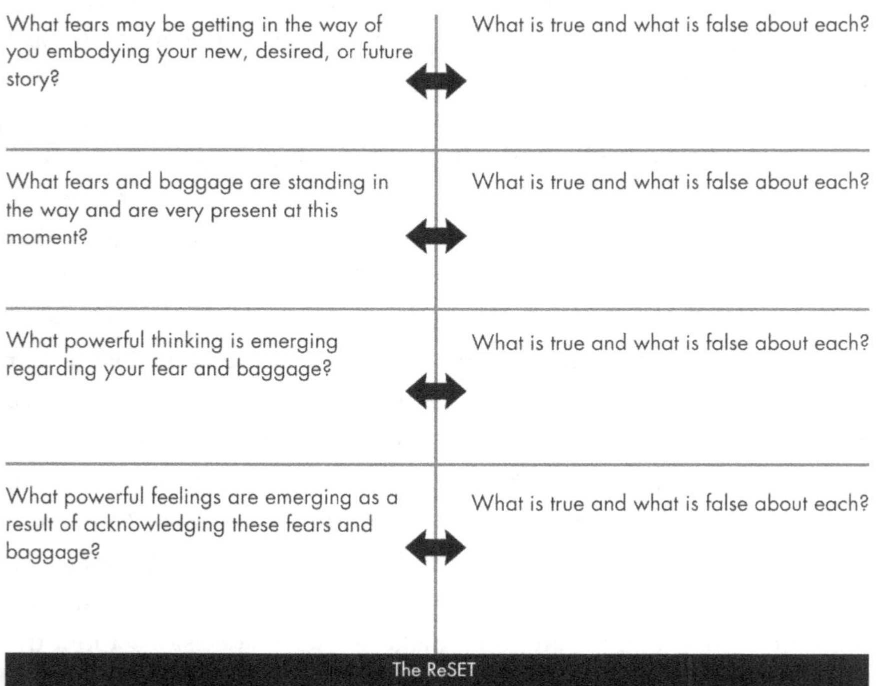

Write a letter to those fears and release them in service of the last part of The ReSET Journey, which positions you for radical reintroduction, celebration, and changing the game.

Use the following template:

Dear (name the specific fears and/or baggage),

I am writing this letter to break up with you. (Share why you are breaking up with it.)

I am letting go and interrupting the following types of thinking, feelings, and actions that served me in my old story but block my ability to celebrate my new embodied story. (List the antiquated thoughts, feelings, and actions that no longer serve you.)

Given my new elevated posture, I embrace the following thoughts, feelings, and actions toward my new and embodied story. (List the new thoughts, feelings, and actions you'll embrace.)

Over the next ninety days, I will take the following strategic action to let go of this fear and baggage toward embodiment posture and stance. (Describe the action in detail.)

I intentionally choose to realign, manage, replenish, or refocus the following labor and energy in service to sustaining, holding, and amplifying this elevated, (Describe the labor and energy in detail.)

When I move in this embodied journey in this elevated posture, the following will be possible, and I will be a game changer, personally and professionally, in the following ways. (Describe the game changer actions and success in detail.)

Love,
(your name)

Next, read the letter aloud to yourself. Hear yourself speaking parts of that journey that are often unspoken. This is also the first acknowledgement of what will be required to move these powerful actions forward. Speaking these unspoken parts of the work gives you permission to release and own your agency and power to choose a different path forward.

Then, share the letter with a trusted friend who can support you with accountability. Read it aloud to them to create critical accountability for each of your commitments. This will provide you with a peer committed to your success on this intentional journey.

Finally, date the letter to be mailed a year from now, and ask a trusted friend to mail it to you on that date. When you receive the letter, it will remind you to celebrate significant milestones you've accomplished since you wrote it. In addition, it will inspire you to reflect, identify powerful lessons you've learned, and consider new possibilities.

Dear ____ (Fear/Baggage),

I am writing this letter to break up with you because _______________

____

____.

I am letting go and interrupting the following types of thinking, feelings,
and actions that served me in my old story but that are/will block my
ability to celebrate my new/desired and embodied story: _____________

____

____.

Given my new elevated posture I embrace the following types of
thinking, feelings, and actions will towards embodying my new/desired
and embodied story ______________________________

____

____.

Over the next 90 days, I will take these steps to prepare and sustain
myself: ____

____

____.

I am prepared to realign/manage/replenish my labor and energy

CALLED FORWARD TO EMBODIMENT

These six powerful words, "You are called forward to embodiment," serve as an important proclamation signifying the significant mastery, integration, normalization, and evolution of the elevated discipline of The Pause, The Pivot, and Forward Stance in your everyday walk. This phrase affirms and amplifies the corresponding courage and leadership needed to move through another aspect of the messy middle toward deep transformation. All the while, you understand the messy middle is a layered and cyclical transformational space, constantly working to move you toward the embodiment of purposeful alignment. Remember calling forward is the conscious invitation to work at a higher vibration, vantage point, and posture to unleash unimaginable impact across each component of your life and walk, ultimately ushering you toward and illuminating your game-changer posture and purpose.

At this stage, you actively demonstrate this higher vibration when you pause, pivot, and intentionally adjust your stance. These actions reposition you and create the optimal conditions for strategic decisions and your best path to your goal. Your ability to seamlessly master and intentionally move through each of these critical disciplines—over and over—not only reveals your unique brand as a game changer, but also sends a strong message that, in every space you choose to occupy, the game will forever be different because you stepped on the floor in all your layers. That simple act reveals your true and authentic story, and your embodied purpose is evident. Your evolution will continue to be front and center in every meeting, space, complex issue, and relationship, highlighting and illuminating your leadership, your story, and the very essence of who you are.

This is the part of the journey where your cumulative actions do the talking to pave a path toward legacy-building work anchored in deep intentionality. In this moment in the game, the voices and actions of others become nonfactors, and you stand toe to toe with what you know is true. You're elevated as the difference maker in your unique role, where you're of service to the world. Your intentional actions reveal a more complete story that further repositions you as a radical storyteller poised and positioned to share a powerful narrative grounded in your new and future stories. The good news is that this narrative will continue to unfold throughout your life.

CHAPTER 8

RADICAL STORYTELLER

From the moment I began to understand the importance of storytelling—as one of the most powerful influences that can shape one's thinking, impact how they feel, and influence their strategic decisions— I was hooked. I constantly thought about the incredible power of stories to shape, distort, redefine, or evoke powerful messages, images, and motivations. This power is a force for change present in the stories we craft and the resulting narrative unleashed to the world.

My desire to understand the deep impact of stories invited me to further explore what it means to be not just a storyteller, but a radical storyteller. This elevated position brings with it an approach unapologetic in redefining, reclaiming, interrupting, and authoring more complete and powerful narratives that accurately reflect your posture as a game changer walking in your aligned purpose.

A radical storyteller uses stories to challenge, speak truth, and foster deep connection through shared narratives from unique perspectives. These narratives drive change and empathy and enable the reclaiming, interrupting, and redefining of personal narratives.

Through the Embodiment Journey, your ability to embrace and create comfort in this role is critical. The reality is that if you don't get comfortable and tell your own story, you relinquish your power and agency to others when they tell it for you. Although often well meaning, they're not authentic and credible narrators of your story; you are!

Embrace Your Role and Take Your Seat

You are a reliable, credible, and effective author and storyteller of your new story.
Omisade Burney Scott

My head spun from the moment this phrase left the lips of Omisade Burney Scott: "You are the most reliable, credible, and effective teller of your story." Her statement created a powerful energy surge and reminder that we each have agency to tell our stories in such a powerful way, and that we should trust our ability to do so in every setting. This moment sparked deep reflection and grappling with this big question: "What does it mean to be a storyteller?"

As I scoured the internet and had deep conversations with friends, filmmakers, and authors, the following was revealed to me: A storyteller serves as much more than a simple narrator; they act as a guardian of a community's culture, history, and collective identity. By weaving together rhythmic language, vivid metaphors, and deep emotional resonance, they create narratives that entertain, enlighten, and offer insightful perspectives of the world.

This raised a powerful question for me about my role as the storyteller of my new story and what parts of my story in this elevated discipline I wanted to highlight, protect, and illuminate as part of a powerful ongoing narrative. These would serve as bright spots as I moved toward radical reintroduction and celebration in the Embodiment Journey. This curiosity continued as I sat in a powerful coaching session, where part of my story centered on the imagery of perfume.

> She said I was perfume.

Halfway through a deep coaching session, my coaching client's commitment to lean in, notice her discomfort, and fight through to name what she wanted in her life amazed me. I invited her to think about leaders she admired, characteristics of their leadership and personality, and how they moved in the world. Unexpectedly, she talked about a recent conference we'd attended together. She described how she watched me move through the crowds, greeting colleagues and old friends. She shared that she watched as I moved in and out of spaces, leaving nuggets of advice, posing big questions to wrestle with and connecting with those around me with ease. She paused and said, "You are like perfume."

As I sat with her simple yet vivid description of me, I thought about the power of perfume, and how it enters the room before you get there and lingers in every space you enter. Perfume can be soft and subtle, leaving a lasting effect as you engage and walk past individuals, sometimes in the air, sometimes directly on their clothes. A good scent leaves an aroma that invites others to ask questions about its brand and origin story. They may want to buy it for themselves or a loved one. Perfume can shift the feel of a room and enable others to relax, pay attention, or be reminded of powerful memories. It even has the power to influence others. Perfume has the ability to ignite fire or create calm in strategic moments. As I sat with her description, I felt such gratitude for the compliment she offered, and I was taken aback by how she saw me.

"It's not just me," she said. "That's how people experience you in the world."

Her offering created a level of awareness and an evolved image of how I have embodied my own story, how I have embodied my purpose at this elevated level, and how I have embodied this game-changer posture. It was yet another voice and evolving image that invited me to continue to get comfortable in my story.

Getting comfortable in your story doesn't mean stagnating. Instead, it calls you to continue to embrace all the layers of who you are and who you're evolving into. This sacred comfort is meant to build your muscles in the reintroduction process of your new story. It's designed to remind you not to recreate an old narrative.

In the process of getting comfortable in your story, you must resist these five threats:

- **Silence.** Resist being silent about this reintroduction and celebration of who you are in this elevated posture.

- **Unlimited proximity and access.** Refuse to give proximity and access to you to the people, places, spaces, or situations not moving toward your embodied posture from a place of truth, growth, reciprocity, and wanting good things for you.

- **Giving away all your energy.** Build your endurance and awareness to negotiate how much energy is expelled and where you shift in your story.

- **The need to create comfort for others.** In the face of toxicity, unhealthy interactions, or behavior designed to distract you from where you're moving, avoid the voice inside you that desires to make others comfortable at the expense of your own comfort and peace.

- **Stagnating and failing to trust yourself.** Normalize pivoting in the face of noticing ongoing patterns, continued growing, and the need for further stretching to avoid becoming stagnant in your journey.

Getting comfortable is a natural movement toward the radical reintroduction of you and the radical celebration of your story. When you embrace this comfort, you truly embrace that you are a reliable author and storyteller of your new story.

I'm curious to know:

- What does getting comfortable with your story look like as you lean into, prepare for, and embrace your role as a radical storyteller?

- Are there places where you need to shift into a Forward Stance to trust yourself and be a reliable and effective radical storyteller of your new story?

- What ongoing stretching and growth are required as you embrace this new role now and beyond this moment?

- Who from your circle of influence can help you set intentions, be accountable, and move past discomfort in the embodiment posture?

Radical Reintroduction

The ReSET propels you forward and repositions you to reintroduce yourself and your new story.

In *Choosing Purposeful Alignment: The Messy Middle of Transformation*, I shared the idea of reintroducing yourself. The reintroduction process is one of the most exciting and one of the scariest moments of your purposeful alignment journey. It's the moment when you choose to unapologetically share all of who you are with the world. It's the moment when you know you'll be celebrated, criticized, or viewed as different, and you're at peace with any of those results. What matters most to you is how you view yourself through the lens of your new story. In this moment of reintroduction, five critical shifts reveal themselves.

Shift #1. Clarity: In this reintroduction, your level of clarity about your purpose peaks, and it's clear to everyone around you. Clarity is such an amazing gift because when you're clear, you can make more concise decisions without the need to apologize, explain, or qualify. The need for approval you once had shifts to seeking counsel from your most trusted truth-tellers, those leading change on the cutting edge, those aligned with your values. In this space, the voices of those who don't matter are quickly drowned out.

Shift #2. Relationships: Healthy and positive relationships are heightened. Your ability to quickly recognize toxic relationships becomes sharper. You're drawn to healthy relationships that foster the creation of intentional space and the interruption of false narratives. These holistic relationships resist complicity in supporting issues and practices that are harmful and perpetuate inequities, and they operate from a place of good intention and honesty, without a hidden agenda. They create safe spaces that resist vilifying and rendering individuals invisible when issues get uncomfortable and hard.

Shift #3. Boundaries: Healthy boundaries right-size your investments across all aspects of your life. This is how you determine what is most aligned. Boundaries allow you to view yourself, the world, and others in ways that enable you to make clear and strategic choices regarding how to move forward. They allow you to attract new opportunities in service to purposeful alignment. Like attracts like.

Shift #4. Commitments: You view your commitment to change differently and embrace curiosity. This enables new awareness and sharpened ability to ask critical questions without judgment or opinion. You think bigger about what's possible and ask questions that influence the thinking of others.

Shift #5. Expectancy: Your expectation is amplified, it is magnified, and it becomes contagious. You desire everyone to thrive and look at everything through the lens of the collective. The expectation that everyone thrives becomes the norm and is a non-negotiable that creates an enormous ripple, which multiplies in the form of new relationships, networks, initiatives, and partnerships.

The reintroduction process is not easy. It is an imperative that has to be named and moved through to experience the benefits of these five core shifts as you reintroduce yourself. You must have a deep belief that the reintroduction is an intentional process of liberation, a stance that could create discomfort in others. This discomfort is real and can manifest as resistance to your story and who you are in a way that you could never have imagined. It's important in these moments to lean into who you are and what you believe could be possible on the other side of the hard space.

In this space, you show up as a mirror for others who have yet to commit to doing their work or are paralyzed by the labor required to move to the other side. Bravery is required and enables you to take your seat as a radical storyteller. This type of bravery cannot be relegated to others; it has to come from deep within you, and you must practice it daily, even in the most difficult moments. As you position and reposition yourself in your new story, you become more comfortable in your Forward Stance and in your ability to reintroduce your story. This begins your radical celebration of that story.

Radical Celebration

You are a reliable author and storyteller of your new story. Embrace being called forward and be in radical celebration of it.

Your powerful new story, aligned with your embodied purpose and new posture of Forward Stance, positions you for a radical celebration.

The Forward Stance moves you into a different type of celebration of your new and evolved story. Remember, Forward Stance requires you to move from an elevated position as an embodied game changer. From this position, you actively and consistently align with your clear purpose and you own the authorship of your new story. This centers purposeful alignment, unapologetically, and allows you to operate at a high vibration visible to all. It's a true celebration, bold, unapologetic, healing, and visible. Here, talking about your evolved story is normalized in every conversation, walk, practice, and engagement that operates from a place of love. This allows you to show up as your best self. In order to be radical in your celebration, you must be poised to do, see, and surrender to it from multiple vantage points.

Radical celebration is a gift and an important step in the final stage of the Embodiment Journey. It's a privileged practice and enables diverse individuals and communities to share space and honor aspects of each other's stories: the wins, struggles, sacrifices, and impacts. Radical celebration honors the power of the collectiveness of our embodied stories. It solidifies that we are stronger, clearer, more impactful, and aligned in a shared line of sight. Radical celebration honors that we all move in our purpose in service to something bigger than ourselves, which creates the right energy to shift and sustain momentous change.

Radical celebration creates the spaciousness to elevate questions, discourse, partnerships, and networks. These are all necessary parts of a critical infrastructure to carry you into the next chapter beyond the embodiment of your story. Radical celebration is the understanding that we are all game changers in our personal and professional lives, not just supporters, advocates, and leaders. We're champions who have uniquely positioned our social, relational, intellectual, and financial capital and cover for each other to enact change. Knitting our collective tables and stories together enables us to sit together and amplify each other's work.

Radical celebration is the giving of our time, talent, treasure, and solidarity to one another. It is the deep belief that "good trouble," as Georgia Congressman John Lewis stated, is necessary. It's needed to enact and inspire meaningful change. Radical celebration creates intentional space to weave a complete story based in truth and celebrate the embodiment of it with one another. With radical celebration, we honor and view each other through the midst of the heavy and important work we do. Radical celebration is how we show up for each other and how we ask honestly, "How can I be of service to you while honoring your new and evolving story?"

Radical celebration is caring for each other and seeing each other's new story from a place of love, joy, respect, and admiration. In this space, we take responsibility for fumbling through the reconciliation processes with one another as we bump up against our own work, hurts, pain points, and fears. As a result, the collective wins because we make space to tackle some of the hardest issues of our lifetime. We normalize processes that allow us to fumble toward repair and build a culture aligned with an embodied purpose and game-changer posture. We choose to occupy this space and normalize this practice, over and over, as we continue the Embodied Journey.

Lastly, radical celebration is setting intentions and accepting the agency to celebrate powerful choices. I have come to understand so deeply, through this experience, that the work of radical celebration is an important and necessary permission as you become a radical storyteller and narrator of your new and elevated story. Are you ready?

I'm curious to know:

- What does it look like as you prepare to radically reintroduce and celebrate your new story?

- Are there places where you need to shift into a Forward Stance around the areas of resistance to fully celebrate who you are in your embodied story, posture, and purpose?

- What ongoing stretching and growth is required in the midst of the celebration and beyond?

- Who from your circle of influence can help you set intentions, be accountable, and move past the discomfort in the embodiment posture?

CHAPTER 9

CALLED FORWARD: FROM PROPOSITION TO EMBODIMENT TO FLOW

You are officially called forward.

I love my late-night talks and early Saturday morning calls with Stephanie. She's my friend, colleague, auntie, mentor, mentee, and second mom all rolled into one. Her voice can be stealth and quiet, while at the same time, powerful. She often repeats the same line to me in our conversations: "To whom much is given, much is required." Each time these powerful words pour from our lips, I hear the echoing of five powerful words: "You are officially called forward."

You are officially called forward with the understanding that calling forward is not a one-time event. The act of calling forward happens in each moment over the course of your life and new evolved story. This official call comes with the expectation that you will intentionally maintain a clear line of sight. This future-focused posture enables you to constantly evolve and consistently resist the pull to move back to the proposition of what could be. You choose to fully stand in who you are in your embodied purpose and game-changer posture.

Called forward marks an important milestone in The ReSET Journey, where you truly understand, embrace, and actively model the responsibility of this type of posture. It's an important milestone, where you unapologetically stand in and embrace your unique position, offering, and role in every space, relationship, body of work, and sector you enter. In this posture, you understand you are the architect of what comes next. Your ability to dream bigger is expanded. At the same time, your capacity to weigh the implications, heighten the success, and gauge choice points is elevated. Reality testing is the intentional work to distinguish your internal thoughts, feelings, and perspective against concrete evidence to see things as they really are. It sets the stage for innovation and an emergent process that invites a practice of test, do, and learn. As a result, you create just enough focused energy and space for new designs.

As an architect in this new posture, you normalize an intentional process to interrupt old stories and narratives. You calmly resist the seductive conversations in your head that can instill fear, paralyze you, and keep you from changing the game. As you take control over the narrative and, ultimately, the story, you align with your embodied purpose and heighten the mental models with the accurate picture of who you are. Those narratives that worked for you last year and in this Called-Forward posture will not work today in your embodied purpose. Every life change requires a ReSET of your story to interrupt disempowering thinking, feelings, and actions and to drop down into powerful thinking, feelings, and actions.

Embodying being a game changer toward purposeful alignment requires ongoing intentionality that keeps you front and center as a radical storyteller in your life. This state of being called forward is not for the weary. In the final chapters of *Choosing Purposeful Alignment*, I shared that this is an ongoing transformation, a posture grounded in a faith walk.

You hold an explicit understanding that you are called forward not by chance. You must be obedient to the calling. And in order to sustain it, you have to be conscious of your flow. To reiterate, flow is a state in which you're aligned in a seamless way, mentally, physically, emotionally, and spiritually. Flow is a sign of your ongoing commitment to honor the transformational process and the lessons learned. Flow requires balance, stance, and energy to sustain you. Flow is necessary to hold yourself—and model for others—the elevated discipline required for the ongoing commitment to purposeful alignment. This energy flow is different from any cadence you have experienced in the past because now you're called forward and maintain the shift from choosing to embodiment. This flow can create a significant ripple effect of choices, impact, relationships, and innovation that will show up for generations to come.

I have such gratitude for my circle of influence for their willingness to walk alongside me, grapple with me, and push me to stretch into and hold this elevated discipline, one that has yielded so much impact and so many invitations into uncharted waters. Thankfully, there has always been support waiting on the other side. These new pathways have revealed the elevated game-changer posture, story, and purpose in ways I couldn't have envisioned.

The Ongoing Invitation

I continue to extend a humble invitation for ongoing and deeper engagement with you and your work. Accepting this invitation will break you open and provide a powerful array of resources to arm you on your journey. This ongoing work requires bravery, community, and support as you continue to make strategic choices and take actions aligned with this embodied posture.

Accept this invitation and join me by taking the following actions:

- Complete the purposeful alignment survey.

- Download the *Aligned Intensive Digital Workbook Series* (English and Spanish versions available).

- Share this book and *Choosing Purposeful Alignment: The Messy Middle of Transformation*.

- Sign up for a series of powerful coaching sessions with me. Coaching is a tool and respects the inextricable link between effective leadership, purpose, and transformational change. It's a vital lever to strategically position leaders to be bolder, more innovative, and future focused.

- Sign up on my website to receive information about events, coaching, offers, and opportunities at indigoinnovationgroup.com

Scan the QR code for additional free resources.

https://indigoinnovationgroup.com/reset-resources | Passcode. ReSET2026!

ABOUT THE AUTHOR

Tracey Greene-Washington is the president of Indigo Innovation Group, a consulting firm dedicated to partnering with leaders and organizations to accelerate transformational change through strategy, leadership development, and systems-level approaches. As a strategic thought partner, advisor, facilitator, strategist, coach, and speaker, Tracey brings to her work more than twenty-five years of experience guiding philanthropic, nonprofit, and business leaders through complex change. Her work helps leaders and teams strengthen culture, build alignment, and lead with purpose during times of transition and growth.

At Indigo Innovation Group, Tracey helps leaders move from awareness to action, bridging the gap between vision and execution. Her approach integrates the disciplines of change leadership, organizational development, change management, and futurism, as she helps organizations navigate complexity and achieve sustainable impact with clarity. Tracey's methodology is rooted in purposeful alignment, ensuring strategy, people, and culture work in concert toward lasting impact.

Before founding Indigo Innovation Group, Tracey held several distinguished leadership roles in philanthropy, nonprofits, and community development. She served as Director of Special Initiatives for the Kate B. Reynolds Charitable Trust, where she led two long-term, place-based initiatives: Healthy Places NC, focused on improving health outcomes in rural counties, and Great Expectations, an early childhood initiative in Forsyth County. Prior to this, she was a Program Officer at the Z. Smith Reynolds Foundation, leading statewide efforts to address the wealth gaps. Earlier in her career, she served as Program Officer and Director of Learning & Evaluation for the National Rural Funders Collaborative, advancing rural community transformation nationwide, and as Director of Technical Assistance, Training & Policy for the South Carolina Association of Community Development Corporations, supporting forty-five CDCs across the state in building local capacity and sustainable development.

Beyond her consulting and coaching work, Tracey is the Founder of CoThinkk, a social change philanthropy committed to advancing economic mobility, education, health, and leadership among communities of color in Western North Carolina. Through strategic investments, network-building, and civic dialogue, CoThinkk has become a model for community-led philanthropy and systems change.

Tracey is also a social entrepreneur and co-owner, with her husband, of No Grease Northlake and No Grease Premium, two businesses that combine enterprise with economic impact. In addition, she serves as Co-CEO of Razored Technologies, alongside her husband Edmund Washington, the CEO. Razored Technologies is an emerging company focused on technology solutions that drive innovation across the grooming industry. Across all her ventures, Tracey's work centers on equipping game-changing leaders to operate with intentionality and boldness in pursuit of their mission.

An award-winning author and speaker, Tracey's first book, *Choosing Purposeful Alignment: The Messy Middle of Transformation*, received the Nautilus Book Award and achieved international bestseller status. In her widely viewed TEDx Talk, "Addressing Complex Social Change—What If?" she challenges audiences to reimagine how they approach change by embracing complexity as a catalyst for innovation and growth.

Over her career, Tracey has been recognized nationally for her leadership and social impact. Her honors include the 2025 50 Women to

KNOW in North Carolina, the 2024 Black Women Give Back Award, 2023 KNOW 100 Women to Know Across America, 2022 Coach Institute for Innovation Impact Award, 2021 Rosa Parks Award, and 2020 Linetta Gilbert Service Award from the Community Investment Network, among others.

Tracey has also served in multiple leadership and governance roles, including Board Chair of EducationNC and The Center for Leadership Innovation, as well as board positions with the Southern Rural Development Initiative, NC Center for Public Policy Research, and the NC Early Childhood Foundation.

Tracey grew up in Asheville, North Carolina, and continues to ground her work in community and purpose, partnering with leaders nationwide to catalyze change, foster alignment, and build the next generation of game-changing leadership. She is guided by a singular purpose: to help others lead with courage, clarity, and purposeful alignment to become the game changers their communities and organizations need most.

ACKNOWLEDGMENTS

This book is dedicated to all the game changers, co-architects, bridge-builders, innovators, visionaries, storytellers, dreamers, weavers, and strategic activators committed to embodiment and the active demonstration of their aligned purpose. To those who are poised as drivers of transformational impact in service to birthing something bigger than themselves. These visionary leaders of intentional impact serve as a catalytic lever, constantly working in both the backdrop and forefront to strategically facilitate intentional, iterative, and emergent change in this moment and every moment moving forward.

A heartfelt thank you to my husband, Edmund Washington, who is an amazing partner and leader in our family and business ventures. His ability to ask critical questions and push my thinking while loving me deeply is so appreciated and is part of the secret sauce that allows me to lean into my work and role to support deep, transformational impact. And to my son, Caleb Dorsett, for his great questions, curiosity, love, and support.

Profound appreciation goes out to my community who pushed me and walked alongside me during this journey. Without this support and help from the collective—friends, family, and philanthropic, nonprofit, W.E.W., and WPO peers and colleagues—I would not have been inspired and committed to evolve and stretch at each critical point of this journey. In particular, Janean Benton, Robin Joiner, Donna Marie-Winn, Towanna Burrous, Aundra Wallace, Tamela Spann, Kathyn Evans, Jennifer Mayer, Barrie Barton, Tamika Mosely,

Veronica Hemmingway, LaRita Barber, Abena Asante, Betty Hines, and countless others have been my rock.

A special thank you to my CoThinkk family for their unapologetic pushing, challenging questions, support, collaboration, and essential moments of softness throughout this journey, particularly Carolina McCready, Tracy Hopkins, and Stephanie Swepson Twitty. Thanks as well to Gladys K. Washington, who taught me so much about what it means to lead and who transitioned into an ancestor this year.

A special thank you to my family, particularly my mother Yvette Jives, who served as a powerful beta reader for my first book and challenged my thinking as that book unfolded, my father, Lonnie Jives, and my siblings, Willie Greene III, Shauntey Jives, and Joe Greene.

What would I have done without my beta readers, Edmund Washington, Julia Darity, Janean Benton, Marcus Walton, Ryan Francis, Garima Grupa, Kristy Tesky, Gary Hubbell, Robin Joiner, Donna Marie Winn, Michelle Sorrells, Lasindra Webb, Jazmin Rogers, and Caleb Owolabi. Their honest critique and feedback helped ensure I spoke to the right audience for this book and ensured clarity and spaciousness for thoughtful reflection to support others who are choosing to walk this journey intentionally. My hope is to not only inspire others to choose purpose but to embrace an elevated discipline and practice to sustain, hold, and evolve their embodiment of it in every aspect of their lives.

9 781971 310046